THE REGULATION AND PREVENTION OF

ECONOMIC CRIME

INTERNATIONALLY

THE REGULATION AND PREVENTION OF
ECONOMIC CRIME
INTERNATIONALLY

Consultant Editor: Jonathan Reuvid

FOREWORD
Tony Baldry
Parliamentary Under Secretary of State
Foreign & Commonwealth Office

PUBLISHED WITH THE SUPPORT OF
The British Foreign & Commonwealth Office Know-How Fund

Titmuss Sainer Dechert

Touche Ross

**KOGAN
PAGE**

First published in 1995

Kogan Page Ltd
120 Pentonville Road
London N1 9JN

© Kogan Page 1995

British Library Cataloguing in Publication Data
A CIP record for this book is available from the British Library.
ISBN 0 7494 1539 8

Typeset by Patrick Armstrong, Book Production Services.
Printed in England by Clays Ltd, St Ives plc.

Contents

Acknowledgements

We are enormously grateful to the Joint Assistance Unit of the Foreign & Commonwealth Office and the Know-How Fund for the financial support and encouragement that made it possible to research and produce this book and to distribute it in the countries of East and Central Europe and the CIS, as well as developing countries worldwide.

We would also like to thank the C2 and F3 Divisions of the Home Office and the Drugs, International Crime and Terrorism Department of the Foreign & Commonwealth Office for their encouragement in guiding us through the mass of UK legislation and European Conventions encompassing the subject matter of Part Two, to Dr Barry Ryder, Dean of Jesus College, Cambridge and Director of CIDOEC, for his invitation to the Editor to attend a part of the Twelfth International Symposium on Economic Crime and, of course, to the contributing authors.

Finally, our appreciation to Tony Baldry, Parliamentary Under Secretary of State at the Foreign & Commonwealth Office, for his Foreword and to Saul M Froomkin, QC, whose brilliant introduction defines the background within which the overall scope and content of the book has been framed.

Jonathan Reuvid

London, June 1995

Foreword

Economic crime is not new. But it is growing, both in incidence and complexity. Hard to detect, it presents the investigator and the prosecutor with a challenge as tough as any other form of crime. The drug cartels can employ the 'best' professional advice, be it witting or unwitting, to launder the proceeds of their crime. Many fraudsters are using state of the art technology to outwit their employers or deceive investors.

Against that background I welcome the publication of this timely and practical book. It highlights the vital importance of sound regulation of industries vulnerable to economic crime, of appropriate empowerment of the regulator, of cooperation between regulators and, by no means least, of the onus on the private sector itself to define, monitor and enforce best practice to deter the menace of economic crime.

The British Government is committed to the fight against all forms of economic crime from corporate fraud to the laundering of the profits of drug traffickers and organised crime gangs. Both of the latter represent a major threat not only to the UK, its citizens and its economy, but to almost every other country in the world. The Foreign and Commonwealth Office is pleased to be associated with this second book in the Kogan Page series and, as with the first, have assisted its publication with finance from our Know-How Fund.

Tony Baldry

Parliamentary Under Secretary of State,
Foreign and Commonwealth Office

Introduction

The International Development of Economic Crime and its Control

Saul M Froomkin QC

Although economic crime has been a phenomenon of commercial life since the days of the Romans, it has become, in the latter half of the 20th century, a growth industry.

In days of yore, the boundaries within which crimes were committed were circumscribed by the distance over which people might reasonably travel by horse, the ports to which they might sail by ship and the borders they had to cross. With the development of sophisticated means of communication, jet travel facsimile machines, the wire transfer of money and new open borders, there are now no barriers to those who would prey on our financial institutions, destroy the economic stability of our commercial enterprises, or corrupt our governments.

Economic crime has become the crime of choice – it is a crime of low risk and high gain. More often than not, little investment is required; access to a fax machine and a telephone are sufficient tools with which to perpetrate massive frauds.

As a result of the virtual eradication of the borders in the European Union, and the desire to allow freer circulation of goods, capital and workers, it is inevitable that criminals too will move freely from jurisdiction to jurisdiction within the Union. It will become simple for the fraudster, corrupt politician and money launderer to travel throughout the Union for the purpose of committing crimes and washing their ill-gotten gains.

With internationalisation of economic crime has come the necessity to legitimise the fruits of crime and accordingly the burgeoning of off-shore banking and bank secrecy legislation. It has been said that such legislation was first enacted in the 1930s by the Swiss to safeguard the legitimate assets of European refugees from confiscation by the Nazis. Since that time, and for very different and perhaps less laudable reasons, many jurisdictions have enacted bank secrecy laws. The South Pacific and the Caribbean, far flung from the international financial centres of the world, have developed off-shore banking into an art form, where invariably the financial institutions are knowingly or unknowingly used, directly or indirectly, for the purpose of concealing the source and the existence of the proceeds of crime. In many instances the laws have been designed to make inaccessible the information required by investigating agencies and defrauded victims.

It has recently been estimated that in excess of US$120 billion is generated each year from the sale of illicit drugs in the US and Europe. These funds must not only be concealed from the prying eyes of the police, but must be legitimised so that the ultimate recipients may enjoy their benefits. The launderer therefore seeks what appear to be normal banking services in international private banking, such as established off-shore trusts, back-to-back loans, and the establishment of off-shore corporate entities as the recipients of these funds.

The demand for off-shore banking licences has become so great that an industry has developed for their purchase and sale. There regularly appear, in publications throughout the world, advertisements for the sale of off-shore banking licences in exotic tropical jurisdictions. Such licences enable the holder not only to proclaim that he or she is the owner of a 'bank', but to transact business worldwide (except in the domicile of the 'bank') as if the entity were a true and legitimate financial institution. These off-shore banks are for the most part mere shells, often with names closely adapted from those of legitimate banks. They are devoid of employees, have no capital base, and are subject to virtually no regulatory control. It goes without saying that such entities have been and are being used for the purpose of perpetrating frauds of all sorts, and to 'pass through' black or grey money. This is particularly the case where the home jurisdiction of the 'bank' has enacted strict secrecy laws prohibiting disclosure of any information regarding accounts or transactions with or by such 'banks'. Accordingly, the use of one of these shell banks provides an effective block to any investigator or regulatory agency once a transaction has reached the portals of such an entity.

Although the licence fees and annual fees may provide well-needed funds for certain off-shore jurisdictions, permitting these so-called 'banks' to operate from within their territories without regulation can only result in continued erosion of their international reputations.

The foreign investigator or regulator attempting to penetrate the walls of secrecy erected around these shell banks will find little incentive for their counterparts off-shore to assist, until a major international financial scandal erupts, bringing down the wrath of the international community upon the heads of those who sell their credibility and integrity to the parasites of the international economic community.

Across Europe a host of investigations and prosecutions of questionable criminal transactions has revealed the scope and depth of the rise in fraudulent and corrupt practices. In France, Germany, Italy and Spain major prosecutions and investigations have commenced, involving losses of billions of dollars, arising out of allegations of corruption, embezzlement and fraudulent practices by some of the biggest names and companies in Europe.

It has been suggested that the economic crisis on the Continent results in a flushing out of existing fraud, and that bad times tempt corporate managers to conceal their business problems. A conservative member of France's parliament was recently quoted as saying that the moral state of European business is reminiscent of the 1980s in the US, and that Europe's march towards freer markets has lacked necessary controls.

The Italian government has uncovered what appears to be systematic corruption within the Guardia di Finanzia, the national tax police. It has been estimated that approximately US$322 billion in tax evasion occurred between 1989 and 1993. It is alleged that many of the major corporate entities, local and international, have traditionally paid bribes to the national tax police to escape the payment of taxes.

With the emergence into free-market reform of East and Central Europe has come the associated problems of all developing countries; namely increased economic crime, money laundering, organised crime, narcotics trafficking, and corruption.

As can be expected, law enforcement agencies in those countries do not presently have either the experience or the personnel to deal with these problems.

In order to combat Mafia-style organised crime in Russia, the Russian government in July 1994 entered into an agreement with the US Federal Bureau of Investigation (FBI) to cope with the emerging crisis. FBI Director, Louis Freeh, warned that US criminals might very well move into Russia to exploit a weak economy during the unsettled period as the Russians move into a full market system. A wave of major organised crime has already been observed in Russia including narcotics trafficking, kidnapping, extortion rackets and corruption. Director Freeh stated that President Yeltsin had acknowledged a very strong and dangerous organised crime presence which the President said could destroy the country's economic institutions.

The prevalence of organised crime and corruption clearly undermines the integrity of the new economic market-place in Russia. The recent collapse of MMM, a Moscow-based financial company with some 10 million shareholders, further eroded the confidence in the three-year-old securities market. It has been estimated that there is some US$40 billion in flight capital overseas, which, assuming a sound, well-regulated and bona fide market-place, could well be returned. Failures such as that of MMM will not build confidence in those who control that capital.

With the absence of any real state boundaries within the former USSR, and the lack of sophisticated accounting procedures and controls, there has been an increase in offences involving the illegal export of raw materials, including strategic resources, industrial products and consumer goods to places outside Russia. The illegal export of raw materials, fuels and non-ferrous metals from Russia into the Baltic and South East Asia has increased dramatically in recent years. The Swedish Customs services has reported that in the months of May to September 1992, 45,000 tonnes of non-ferrous metals were exported from Russia through Estonia into Scandinavia. The consequent loss to Russia in customs duties was estimated at US$9 million.

The international community, faced with this pandemic plague attacking the very foundations of its financial institutions, sucking the life-blood of its economies, and subverting the integrity of its governments, is slowly recognising the need for international cooperation. In 1991 the European Community Finance Ministers agreed to make the laundering of drug money a crime within the Community. A key feature of the declarations passed pursuant to the agreement was the obligation imposed upon banks to ascertain the identity of customers carrying out transactions in excess of £10,000. The agreement only applies to money gained from drug trafficking, and each member state must enact legislation that meets the requirements of the principles set out in the directive.

Effective from 1 January 1994, a joint US/UK task-force was established to investigate fraud and other financial crimes including money laundering. The task-force, made up of two agents from the FBI and two from New Scotland Yard, is based in Miami. The focus of this joint effort will be on the British Dependencies in the Caribbean, the Cayman Islands, Montserrat, Anguilla, the British Virgin Islands and the Turks and Caicos Islands. It is hoped that this team approach will alleviate the bureaucratic red tape normally involved in multijurisdiction investigations.

One of the earliest and most progressive steps was taken in 1988 by the G10 countries (United States, United Kingdom, Belgium, Canada, France, Italy, Japan, the Netherlands, Sweden and Switzerland) and Luxembourg on their adoption of the Statement of Principles of the Basel Committee on Banking Regulations and Supervisory Practices. The directive formulated by the bank supervisors of those jurisdictions urges financial institutions to implement procedures to prevent their facilities from being used in the process of money laundering. As a result of this coming together of most of the nations where major financial entities of the world are located, subsequent conventions and international directives have been implemented.

In September 1992, the United Kingdom became the first country to ratify the Council of Europe Convention on the Laundering of the Proceeds from Crime. The Convention was also signed by Luxembourg, Bulgaria, Greece and Australia and by Austria, Belgium, Cypress, Denmark, France, Germany, Ireland, Italy, the Netherlands, Portugal, Spain, Sweden and

Switzerland. The Convention is concerned with the laundering of the proceeds of all forms of criminal activity, including arms trafficking, terrorism, tax evasion and drug trafficking. It is expected to improve international cooperation between not only Council of Europe member states, but also with other countries invited to ratify the Convention, including the United States, Canada and Australia.

The indications of international cooperation are certainly encouraging. However, until such time as sufficient funding and manpower are made available, until specialised training in economic crime becomes a high priority, and until real government commitment is demonstrated rather than political posturing, the crisis will not be resolved.

Historically, as regards economic crime, a *laissez-faire* attitude has prevailed in most Western countries. Secret commissions were frowned upon but ignored for the most part; political contributions for expected returned favours were the norm, and until very recently insider dealing was considered as a sport.

There are many who are of the view that governmental intervention will only adversely affect the market-place, promote bureaucratic growth, and force those who are prone to commit crimes merely to find other means to 'beat the system'.

Financial institutions which have been defrauded often refuse to bring the matter to the attention of the police for fear that public disclosure will result in their customers questioning the adequacy of the institution's security systems. It is only when a banking scandal reaches monumental international proportions, such as the results of the BCCI débâcle, that those concerned are forced to sit up and take notice.

In other areas, such as evasion of taxes and breaches of exchange control regulations, views appear to be changing in the international community. It was, and is, a basic tenet of international law that one nation is not obliged to enforce the fiscal policy of another nation. Accordingly, fiscal offences were not normally extraditable, and international cooperation was rarely extended to the investigation of such crimes. More recently, policy makers in many jurisdictions are questioning the rationale behind the principle. The United States, which has no exchange control restrictions, is not concerned with flight capital coming out of India or Africa. The main crisis facing the US is drug trafficking. On the other hand the use and abuse of drugs is not the greatest concern of Africa and India. It is the outflow of hard currency which destroys their economic stability.

Capital flight normally results from anticipated political or economic uncertainty, or perceived excessive tax rates. As a result, complex but highly effective underground banking systems have emerged such as the Hawala in India, and the Fei Ch'ien in Chinese communities. These systems are virtually impenetrable by outsiders, and are the mechanisms by which incredible sums of money, both illicit and licit, flow. An international survey conducted on behalf of India disclosed that Indian Hawala operations were spread from the Philippines and Hong Kong in the East, to Singapore and Sri Lanka, Oman and Dubai in the Middle East, and the UK, Europe and the US. The capital involved was estimated at US$10 billion. Obviously these underground banking systems are also employed by those who must legitimise or conceal the proceeds of their illegal activities.

The detection, investigation and successful prosecution of the economic criminal is difficult enough for those responsible for it in the developed countries. The cases are generally complex and multijurisdictional, requiring not only dedication and commitment of the investigating agencies and their governments, but the expertise, manpower and funding necessary to undertake the task. Developing countries face an insurmountable task in this regard. The officials of many of these governments, as a result of a combination of factors including a morality accepting of corruption and the existence of low wages, are themselves corrupt or corruptible and have no incentive to change the situation. Many governments are loath to delve into allegations of massive fraud and corruption committed by their predecessors for fear that their successors may be inclined to do the same.

These new nations, whose economies are fragile and whose expertise in the field is limited or non-existent, are ripe candidates for the international fraudsters of the world. These parasites of the international community move into emerging nations as did the carpetbaggers of old, promising to develop industries and to provide venture capital. Instead, every scam known to humanity, and some newly developed ones constructed for the occasion, are perpetrated on naive and unsophisticated bureaucrats. For example, the savings of millions of Russians were wiped out in the collapse of MMM in a classic pyramid scheme.

Virtually all the former eastern bloc countries are now suffering from substantial increases in economic crime committed by locals and by outsiders, who are all taking advantage of the inadequacy of the investigation and prosecution agencies now in place. With the best of intentions in the world, few of the newly developed and developing nations can afford the manpower and monetary drain of their resources to investigate a major international fraud. Few of these nations have either the expertise or the financial ability to mount such an operation. The magnitude of the problem becomes apparent when one considers that by a Special Decree of the President of Russia in 1992, and a subsequent ruling of the government, a budget was approved for 7,800 new judges and 3,500 specialists. Even more frustrating is the impossibility of tracing and repatriating the billions of dollars stolen or illegally removed from these countries.

There is, however, cause for hope. Few of us would even have thought that in our lifetime we would see an article in the *New York Times* entitled 'Old enemies now allied against crime – US and Russia sign pact on policing' (6 July 1994). Dozens of mutual legal assistance treaties, joint task-forces, bilateral and multilateral agreements are now in force, all designed to demonstrate an international commitment to fight multijurisdictional economic crime.

Workshops, seminars and symposia on international economic crime are being held around the world, and are well attended by investigators, officials and regulators. At the Twelfth International Symposium of Economic Crime held at Jesus College, Cambridge in September 1994, almost 500 delegates from some 65 countries attended over the course of the week.

The complexity and diversity of the crimes considered under the rubric 'economic crime' is so vast and chameleon-like as to require constant updating by those involved in its detection, investigation and prosecution. Specialised training and networking are vital to all those engaged in the challenge of eradicating the plague which has befallen us.

Accordingly, a handbook such as this will be an invaluable

aid in understanding the scope of the problem and in gaining some insight into how to cope with it.

The Contributors

Tony BALDRY is Parliamentary Under Secretary of State, Foreign & Commonwealth Office.

Rowan BOSWORTH-DAVIES is a Senior Consultant with City law firm Titmuss Sainer Dechert and Honorary Research Fellow at the Centre for Police and Criminal Justice Studies, Exeter University.

John FORBES is Senior Manager, of the Commercial Investigations Group, Touche Ross & Co, United Kingdom.

Saul FROOMKIN QC is Chairman of the Centre for International Documentation on Organised and Economic Crime (CIDOEC), former Attorney-General of Bermuda and Director of Criminal Law, Federal Government of Canada, now Senior Litigation Partner, Mello, Hollis, Jones and Martin (Bermuda).

Martyn JONES is a member of the City Regulatory Panel and Working Party on Internal Control of the CBI; he is also a member of the Auditing Committee of the Institute of Chartered Accountants in England and Wales and of the Audit Procedures Task Force of Deloitte Touche Tohmatsu International.

Jonathan REUVID is a writer of business books and consultant editor to Kogan Page Ltd, and an international business consultant specialising in joint venture development, technology transfers and market research in China.

Graham SALTMARSH is an Honorary Research Fellow, at the Centre for Police and Criminal Justice Studies, Exeter University.

Sir Kenneth WARREN is Former Chairman of the House of Commons Select Committee on Trade and Industry.

Part One
DIAGNOSIS

1.1
Definition and Classification of Economic Crime

Rowan Bosworth-Davies and Graham Saltmarsh

Introduction

Property is theft.
Pierre-Joseph Proudhon 1809–65

At the heart of all Western, free-market capitalist economies lies a fundamental paradox. It is identified by the need to provide the greatest degree of commercial freedom for the market to enable entrepreneurial business to flourish; while, at the same time, ensuring that those whose criminal activities would subvert and undermine the commercial effectiveness of those markets are denied access to the benefits which that very freedom allows. It is one of the great ironies of Western capitalism that in so many cases, the most apparently innovative and entrepreneurial financial schemes, which are the most attractive to investors, are all too often the brainchild of the white-collar criminal.

For countries whose free-market economies are still evolving, it is extremely difficult to strike the delicate balance between the imposition of too great a degree of bureaucratic regulation, which has a tendency to inhibit new commercial development, and deliberately refraining from the introduction of any prudency legislation at all, thus allowing their emerging markets to become infiltrated by criminally corrupting influences who offer tempting short-term profits, but with accompanying long-term damage and subversion. Nevertheless, it must be recognised at an early stage that criminal infiltration of the commercial infrastructure of society is one of the quickest ways of ensuring the ultimate corruption of the social and political fabric, with all the inherent implications that such a scenario possesses for the very basis of a free democracy.

> The present devastation of the social, political and economic fabric of the developing world through, among other things, the phenomenon of international economic crime is hardly perceived, let alone acknowledged. There is compelling evidence that some national economies ... are coming under such an attack from organised crime groups and those engaged in economic crime that their political institutions have been significantly weakened and corrupted.[1]

Economic crime, by the very disparate nature of its component activities, is incapable of simple definition. In this chapter, we are going briefly to examine illustrations of the kind of activities which assist in undermining the commercial effectiveness of the capitalist free market, in an attempt to provide a working definition of economic crime. The reader should, however, bear in mind that the views expressed here are our own and are not necessarily those which might be expressed by the average commercial market practitioner, and they do not necessarily represent, in any way, the views of our employers. We are not business people, but law enforcers and legal practitioners who have spent our working lives observing, investigating and prosecuting the criminal activities of the dark side of the commercial paradox, and, of necessity, our opinions will be considered by many to be wholly polarised. That being so, it would be unduly naïve for us to ignore the lessons that in excess of 50 years of collective experience have taught us; and when business people or financial practitioners accuse us of displaying a lack of understanding or sympathy for the peculiar needs of the entrepreneurial market, in our view it is worth remembering that the greatest exponents of criminality in business are business people themselves. Any investigator who is required to investigate an allegation of economic loss within the commercial environment should start by immediately suspecting those who have reported the crime.

White-collar criminality in business is expressed most frequently in the form of misrepresentation in financial statements of corporations, manipulation in the stock exchange, commercial bribery, bribery of public officials directly or indirectly in order to secure favourable contracts and legislation, misrepresentation in advertising and salesmanship, embezzlement and misapplication of funds, short weights and measures and misgrading of commodities, tax frauds, misapplication of funds in receiverships and bankruptcies. These are what Al Capone called 'the legitimate rackets.' These and many others are found in abundance in the business world.[2]

Corruption (government and corporate)

Economic crime directly undermines the stability of society. It can lead to political and social instability and in extreme cases dissatisfaction with and dissatisfaction within a society that permits such activities to continue. Economic crime undermines confidence in the integrity and thus the efficiency of such mechanisms as may exist for the proper allocation of economic resources. This will sooner or later lead to a lessening of confidence in the competence and perhaps even the integrity of those who are charged with the proper functioning of the state's economic apparatus.[3]

Corruption in public life is a good example of the free-market paradox identified earlier.

Corruption is behaviour which deviates from the formal duties of a public role because of private-regarding (personal, close family, private clique) pecuniary or status gains; or violates rules against the exercise of certain types of private-regarding influence. This includes such behaviour as bribery (use of a reward to pervert the judgement of a person in a position of trust); nepotism (bestowal of patronage by reason of ascriptive relationship rather than merit); and misappropriation (illegal appropriation of public resources for private-regarding uses).[4]

Paying commission to an intermediary who facilitates the marketing of one's products may be thought to be an acceptable practice, but when that commission is being paid to a public official in the ordinary function of his or her office, it becomes a criminal act. One of the pre-requisites of a free market is the need for competition, but this creates a climate of uncertainty for producers who, in order to minimise the degree of uncertainty, or to obtain an unfair advantage over a fellow competitor, will resort to acts of bribery. The person receiving the bribe is usually in a position to influence the decision-making process; to favour one supplier over another; to grant an export licence; to facilitate the early completion of necessary documentation; or to impose additional bureaucratic burdens on a competitor. In many countries, bribery in public life is endemic and it becomes hard, if not impossible, to conduct business without recourse to the payment of bribes.

> Corruption is so central to the politics of African nations such as Cameroon, Zaire and Nigeria that it is unlikely that anybody living in those states could avoid encountering it . . . in many African states it is 'systematic' in the sense that it has become the norm in government and administration . . . It can be seen that systematic corruption involving regular misappropriation and misuse of public funds could well play a major part in reducing already poor nations to a state of economic crisis.[5]

Ingo Walter identifies four distinct categories of payment which possess corrupt characteristics:

- *Bribes*: significant payments to officials with decision-making powers   to convince them to do their jobs improperly.
- *Grease*: 'facilitating' payments to minor officials to encourage them to   do their jobs properly.
- *Extortion:* payments to persons in authority to avoid damage from hostile actions on the part of unions, criminals, utilities, 'renegade troops' and the like.
- *Political contributions:* payments to political parties linked to favours or threats of retribution in case of non-payment.[6]

The effect of such payments means that ordinary commercial life soon becomes undermined because the bribes have to be paid for, and they are inevitably passed on by the payer of the bribe to the customer, who ends up paying more for inferior goods. At the same time, the corrosive effect of institutionalised corruption permeates every level of society, leading to the growth of a cynical disregard for such inchoate subjects as commercial morality, public-sector ethics or the rule of law.

> Economic crime is invariably associated with corruption, which of course, represents an even more direct attack on the integrity of the state and its institutions. The commission of many forms of economic crime necessitates at some level corruption of officials. The vast amounts of money that are often involved enable protection and facilitation to be purchased. There are, sadly, countries where corruption has become almost endemic. Even those who, whilst not corrupt in the conventional sense of the word, are prepared to facilitate economic crime by others, are on a slippery slope.[7]

The abuse of aid programmes

Increasingly since the Second World War, the more developed countries of the Northern hemisphere have provided financial and economic aid programmes to underdeveloped nations in what we have conveniently come to call the 'Third World'. A proportion of the aid supplied has been donated by religious and social welfare charities, who draw their funding to a large extent from voluntary contributions given by well-intentioned private donors. These funds are administered in the beneficiary state by representatives of the charity or welfare group and are usually associated with religious or charitable purposes, locally incorporated.

By far the greatest proportion of aid funds, however, are provided by government agencies, and the terms under which such aid packages are given are very often associated with parallel, reciprocal agreements such as the supply of arms or other military hardware; the provision of 'political advice or consultancy'; or the guaranteeing by the recipient government of the suppression of the political ambitions of groups whose aims are perceived to be antithetical to those of the donor state.

Similar payments to those made in the Iran/Contra affair have, in the past, become the subject of judicial oversight and investigation when the discovery of their payments and the uses to which they have been put have become public knowledge within the donor nation. More recently in 1991, following a major fraud trial in Israel, US Department of Defense auditors, examining payments made by US companies in contracts in Egypt and Israel, uncovered widespread evidence indicating that US contractors might have improperly used Foreign Military Financing funds to pay unauthorised commissions; to reimburse foreign officials for unauthorised travel expenses; and to make unlawful payments for items which were not of US manufacture.

In so many cases, foreign aid payments have been looked upon as a convenient source of funding for dictators, both to enrich themselves and to reward their political supporters, and in many cases the systematic abuse of aid programmes is merely a widely practised adjunct to political corruption. Looting the State Treasury, whether by pocketing the taxes or stealing the foreign aid payments, are synonymous activities.

> At the annual meeting of the IMF and the World Bank in Berlin in September 1988, a German banker responded to proposals for higher aid to Third World debtor states by saying; 'I have not worked 16 hours a day for 40 years so that Third World politicians can salt away fortunes in Zurich.[8]

Ingo Walter recites a list of the huge sums salted away by various dictators. Nicaragua's former head, Anastasio Somosa, 'liberated' at least $500 million before being deposed in 1979. Haile Selassie was worth an estimated $15 billion in foreign banks at the time of his death. Former President Mobutu of Zaire was estimated simply to have transferred his country's $4 billion foreign aid borrowings straight into his Swiss bank accounts, while the Marcoses of the Philippines were described as indulging in 'what can only be described as the unprecedented plunder of a nation'.[9]

The terms under which foreign aid contributions are now being made are subject to a far greater degree of supervisory oversight by donor nations and financing agencies. This oversight can take the form of the withholding of cash or credits if the receiving state is perceived to be lax in introducing relevant fiscal reforms or implementing democratic structures. In November 1993, Spain threatened to withhold $15 million from an aid programme to Equitorial Guinea if its first democratic elections were not observed to be free and fair. The West African country, which is almost entirely dependent on foreign aid, including £45 million from the European Union, could well find itself financially isolated if the economic cooperation, which has to be renegotiated annually, is withheld in the face of perceived electoral corruption. Providing the much-needed hard currency can become subject to rigid pre-conditions. The World Bank $24 billion aid package for Russia was carefully structured in order for it to be targeted at the most pressing Russian economic problem areas.

> In an attempt to minimise fraud and corruption, a system of reimbursement will apply: the central bank will be reimbursed by the World Bank only against receipts for imports of approved goods. These do not include alcohol, tobacco, nuclear materials or jewellery.[10]

Customs and excise fraud

Sovereign countries, with the very few exceptions of the free-port areas, impose import tariffs on goods being brought within their jurisdiction. Customs duties imposed on imported goods provide the leading form of indirect taxation, and attempts to circumvent the collection of such payments are punished severely. Other reasons for imposing tariff barriers are to prohibit the importation of articles which are considered to pose a specific threat to the host nation, whether agricultural, such as the importation of certain kinds of plants into the United States; social, as in the importation of pornographic video films or magazines; or specifically criminal, such as the importation of restricted narcotics. Wherever a demand for specific commodities exists, governments will always seek to impose tariffs on imported goods, both as a means of raising revenue and, to a lesser extent, to protect home-based industries from cheap foreign competition.

Other forms of customs-type fraud include the attempts made by fraudsters within an economic community, such as the European Union, to obtain unlawful payments of agricultural subsidies based upon the production of forged documents, evidencing the production of non-existent commodities; or inflated payments for the underweight export of strategic goods. Fraud in such areas represents a considerable drain on the budgetary resources of the EU and, indeed, the ease with which such fraud-

ulent claims can be made and the sums of money which are theoretically obtainable have made such frauds an irresistable source
of financing for organised criminal entities.

The European Commission's 1992 report on fraud within the
Community disclosed that reported fraud totalled Ecu 269.9m
(£213.8m), 44 per cent of that figure relating directly to illicit
farm subsidy claims. These figures, however, represent only those
frauds which were reported, and by 1993 a Community report
was estimating that the *total* amount of fraud being committed
was probably in the region of £4 billion a year, mainly at the
expense of the common agricultural policy budget and loss of
income from VAT and customs duties.

Parallel trading or 'grey-market' dealings provide another form
of revenue-style frauds, although by far the greatest cause for
concern over this technique is expressed by the producers of those
goods which are most commonly the subject of parallel trading
operations. Producers of luxury consumer items such as perfumes,
cosmetics or designer-label products go to considerable lengths
to maintain the price structures of their products in different
markets. The unit cost of producing a bottle of perfume or an
aftershave lotion bears no resemblance to the price charged to
the end-user, and the degree of profit achieved by the manufac-
turer can be considerable. Such items, hyped by slick advertising
campaigns, become widely sought after and part of their
'mystique', which assists in maintaining their price profile, is
achieved by restricting the number of retailers who are authorised to sell the product.

Nevertheless, the price which can be charged in an exclusive,
New York Fifth Avenue boutique is very different from the price
which could be expected from a retail outlet in Lagos, Delhi or
Bucharest. This does not mean that the retailers will not seek
to infiltrate potentially lucrative, developing markets with their
products, but they will do so at discounted prices, designed to
reflect the potential spending ability of their target market. Stocks
of their product shipped to this market sector will differ, not in
content, but in identifiable package design, style of presentation
and method of advertising, in order to enable the host producer
to be able to differentiate between the product being sold in the
highest-price markets, and that being sold in the developing

markets. The parallel trader exists to purchase large quantities of the goods designated to be sold solely in the low-price market, and to divert those goods to the warehouses of wholesalers operating in the high-price retail sector, enabling them to take advantage of the lower prices charged for the bulk purchase, to undercut the recommended retail price and to discount the product at a rate which still ensures a healthy profit. For glaringly obvious reasons, the manufacturers resent such activities, and go to great lengths to prohibit and prevent such conduct.

Corporate fraud: theft and false accounting

> Well, as through this world I've rambled,
>   I've seen lots of funny men,
>   Some rob you with a six-gun,
>   Some with a fountain pen.
> *Woody Guthrie, 'Pretty Boy Floyd'*

Crime in business of all kinds, or what we shall for greater simplicity call 'white-collar crime', is the inevitable concomitant of business, trading and commerce, and has long been an under-researched phenomenon. The American sociologist Edwin Sutherland first coined the phrase 'white collar' criminality, which he described as: 'A crime committed by a person of respectability and high social status in the course of his occupation'.[11]

Ever since the lawful existence of the limited liability company was developed in the nineteenth century, frauds within companies and frauds committed by corporate entities have become a feature of commercial life. All commercial activities are based on financial risk, and the existence of the limited liability company enables the entrepreneur to undertake those risky commercial activities which are designed to generate profit, secure in the knowledge that his or her financial downside is limited to the amount of authorised capital with which the company is capitalised. Such companies can be easily formed; indeed, the nature of Western free-market commercialism deliberately makes it easy for innovative business people to form such companies, in an attempt to facilitate the freedom of the market to conduct profitable business. However, the very ease with which such companies can be formed means that the crook, the con artist and the commercially incompetent can become company directors with the same ease and simplicity.

In his excellent book, *Business Crime – Its Nature and Control* Michael Clarke defines the dilemma:

> Members of business organisations are protected from detection by a veil of privacy. This is formally and legally the case in respect of the limited company form, which is designed to protect commercial confidentiality and not to give information away to competitors. But privacy is also inherent in the relatively complex and specialised work and context of the organisation . . . It is thus only too easy for individuals or groups within an organisation to shield misconduct from prying eyes and to manipulate outputs so that all appears to be normal.[12]

Once under the protection of a corporate veil, commercial activities which are intended to result in a criminal outcome can be undertaken in exactly the same way as honest business, secured by the fact that their dishonest identification will be difficult to obtain until the damage has been caused, the profits secured and hidden, and the guilty individuals are far away from the scene of the crime. This is yet another example of the free-market paradox referred to earlier.

> Many of these activities are not always immediately defined and recognised as crime, particularly those which are regarded as normal, acceptable and legitimate business practices. The line between acceptable and unacceptable, legal and illegal practices is consequently blurred and constantly shifting.[13]

The most common fraudulent activity encountered is fraudulent trading or 'long-firm fraud', or, to use the American description, 'phoenix' or 'bust-out' companies, where a company is permitted to obtain large quantities of goods on credit, on what appear to be ordinary commercial terms, the supplies being secretly rerouted to other corporate entities or sold at knock-down prices, and the proceeds from the sales being passed back to the controllers of the fraud, whose names or identities in most cases do not appear anywhere in the company documentation. The greatest difficulty is being able to differentiate the deliberate operation of such a company from the activities of a wholly legitimate operation which falls upon hard times owing to economic recession or a falling-off in commercial demand for its products. Once the proceeds from the crime have been secured, the directors of the company allow it to be liquidated, at a complete loss to the creditors, and then they are in a position to start another company in another town, using the same methods.

The losses caused by commercial fraud are extremely difficult to calculate. Fraud is an under-reported crime and those statistics which are capable of determination are estimated to represent approximately 70 per cent of the total amount of fraud committed. During the year 1992–93, the British Serious Fraud Office was investigating fraud cases whose total losses exceeded £5,300 million. Over a third of the cases being investigated involved allegations of theft or false accounting within corporate entities. In the year 1993–94, the figures had risen and the aggregate value of the alleged frauds under investigation was £6,000 million, of which 31 per cent of the cases involved frauds on companies.

The sheer volume and the prevalence of such economic criminal offences within the company commercial sector represent a significant threat to the commercial reputation of financially developed nations, and raise questions as to their fitness to continue as an international centre from which to conduct business. The existence of such crimes in a developing economy or newly emergent democracy represent a serious threat to their future political stability. As Rider succinctly puts it:

> Another reason why economic crime is a matter of concern to us all is that it represents an uneconomic dissipation of scarce resources. Furthermore, it allows those engaged in economic crime to compete on an unfair basis with those who are prepared to remain within the constraints of the legitimate business world. Where economic crime is allowed to continue seemingly unchecked, it is small wonder that attitudes within the business community will change and there will be a tendency to illegality, undermining the social values of that state.[14]

Bank fraud

All free-market economies are based to a large extent on trust; indeed, without that degree of trust, it is doubtful whether many of the instruments of free-market economics could work successfully. At the heart of that trust relationship lies the reputation of the banking sector. All international trade is conducted on a documentary basis: bills of exchange, certificates of deposit, bills of lading, letters of credit, cheques, banker's drafts, telegraphic transfers and collateralised lending, to name but a few of the financial documentary services provided by banks. The proffering of an acceptable form of such documentation in a commercial transaction implies that the profferer has the authority to issue the document; and further, it implies that there will be funds available in the bank to meet the terms of the document when it is presented. On that basis, and in the full knowledge that the clearing bank will pay upon presentation of the document, trillions of dollars worth of commercial transactions are undertaken daily.

On a personal level, without a high degree of trust in the reputation and long-term future of their bank, private clients would find it very difficult to continue to manage their increasingly complex financial arrangements. The range of commercial services now offered by banks to private customers goes way beyond the mere provision of a savings facility. It is the reputation of the banks, both international and local, for integrity, honesty and fair dealing which enables this business to be transacted. Bank fraud undermines that integrity and it goes some way to explaining why, in so many cases, when banks discover that they have been the victim of a fraud, they will keep the details of the losses to themselves and make up the deficit out of their reserves, rather than admit that they have been defrauded, for fear of shaking confidence in their integrity.

Apart from the most obvious kinds of fraudulent activity to which the banking sector is exposed and to which it is well attuned – cheque and credit card fraud (using stolen, forged or, increasingly, counterfeit credit cards to obtain goods, cash or services) and forged credit documentation – the banks are increasingly concerned about the egregious use of their computer systems by dishonest employees or criminal outsiders to obtain cash, and we shall look at this aspect in greater detail in a later section.

One of the main areas of concern for the world's banks, however, is advance-fee and other related documentary credit frauds, because these activities strike at the very heart of the trust relationship. These have been joined in recent years by what are called 'prime bank instrument frauds', a new technique which has developed around the perpetration of a belief in a mythical, highly secretive international banking operation which purportedly enables investors to buy and sell prime bank guarantee paper, prime bank notes, and standby letters of credit. Some of the tales told about this facility are so fantastic that it amazes us that anyone falls for them, but they do. Talks abound of the 'Seven Grand Masters' of the US Federal Bank, who reportedly are the only people in the world permitted to issue prime bank paper and whose identities are kept a closely guarded secret, but who just happen to have authorised the man offering the deal to conduct this business on their behalf!

The criminal skills of the prime bank and advance-fee fraudster represent the epitome of the professional confidence-trickster's abilities. The advance-fee fraudster is able to operate because of the existence of individuals, companies and, indeed, Third World countries, who for reasons of their credit-risk status are unable to obtain loan funding from the usual, legitimate sources of finance and who are increasingly drawn to the services offered by 'lenders of last resort' or 'non-status loan brokers', and who in so many cases find themselves being defrauded by professional advance-fee fraudsters.

The fraudster represents himself as being able to access sources of investment funding, very often at highly attractive rates. He provides assurances to the victim that the institution which he intends to approach for the funding will be in a position to supply the necessary capital, usually in the form of letters of undertaking, drawn up in most cases on the letterhead of the banking institution itself and written in its house style. If necessary, the fraudster will have access to a large amount of 'flash cash' held in a briefcase or safety-deposit box, which he will show the prospective victim as proof that he can acquire the necessary sums. The core of the deal involves the creation of a large quantity of official-looking documentation, setting out the terms of the loan; its interest rate; its repayment schedule and its penalty clauses, together with details of the advance payments required from the victim to defray the necessary administrative expenses; the negotiating fees; the 'goodwill' factoring facility; and any other meaningless, but impressive-sounding jargon which the con-man can dream up.

The payment of the advance fee by the victim is the signal for the criminal and his accomplices to disappear, leaving behind them a victim who in many cases – particularly if he is the Finance Minister of a newly emerging democracy who has introduced his newly acquired banking consultant to his Head of State, who may have entertained him lavishly at the Presidential palace – will be only too willing to keep quiet about the fees the Treasury has paid when the funds to finance the building of the dam or hydro-electric scheme fail to arrive on time.

International banks fear the activities of such fraudsters because, in so many cases, the documentation used to carry out the fraud is genuine, having been acquired from the individual bank concerned by a ruse or trick. In one case we saw, the under-manager of a London branch of a State Bank of a Third World nation became the victim of one such fraudster, who approached him on the pretext of discovering if the bank would be able to provide stand-by letters of credit. On being assured that such business was an everyday function of the bank, once it had received the necessary cleared funds in its accounts, the con-man asked the young banker to provide him with a letter confirming the terms of such business. The ambitious banker willingly supplied the document, in the form of words dictated by the fraudster and written in the house style of the bank and on its own letterhead. He even placed the letter in an unsealed envelope so that his valuable potential client could carry it away from the bank premises.

The letter and its envelope were then used by the fraudsters to re-create exact copy documents, together with a large quantity of commercial documentation, again on the letterhead of the bank. They reappeared some months later in the form of a series of confirmed financing agreements which had been used to underwrite a multi-million dollar bond-financing arrangement in the US. The American losers, who had relied on the authenticity of the bank documents to support their trust in the project in which they had invested their money, sought to sue the bank in London for its negligence in permitting such a document to be supplied in the circumstances.

Among financial institutions within a free-market economic system, banks are the most vulnerable to infiltration, economic subversion and criminal attack. A journalist once asked Willy Sutton, an infamous American bank robber, why, despite all the risks and dangers involved, he continued to rob banks. Sutton's answer provides the clue to understanding why banks will always be the target of the criminal, whether armed robber or fraudster. He said, 'Because that's where they keep the money!'

Investment/securities fraud

There is not a man but will own 'tis a complete system of knavery, that 'tis a trade founded in fraud, born of deceit and nourished by trick, wheedle, forgeries, falsehoods and all sorts of delusions.
Daniel Defoe, The Anatomy of Change Alley

Defoe's elegant eighteenth-century words, parodying as he called it 'the pernicious art of stock-jobbing', prove that fraud in the securities market is a subject as old as the markets themselves. Indeed, these markets are symptomatic of the capitalist paradox, because while they exist to enable individuals with money to invest, to trade financial securities in a free, open and public manner, the decision to buy or sell a particular security is based, in many cases, upon nothing more than a representation of its future value, made by a promoter of the share itself. Therefore the potential for a fraudulent share offering to be made is very high, and it is with the aim of preventing fraud in the sale of securities that all mature free-market economies design their securities legislation.

Such fraud-prevention activities cannot be brought to bear on the determination of the specific worth of an individual stock offering, however, as this would impose an artificial standard on the working of a free commercial market. In other words, it is axiomatic in free-market economies that investors must be free to make imprudent commercial decisions which act to their financial detriment. The US Securities and Exchange Commission describes the paradox in this way:

> It should be understood that the securities laws were designed to facilitate informed investment analyses and prudent and discriminating investment decisions by the investing public. It is the investor, not the Commission who must make the ultimate judgement of the worth of the securities offered for sale. The Commission is powerless to pass upon the merits of securities; and assuming proper disclosure of the financial and other information essential to informed investment analysis, the Commission cannot bar the sale of securities which such analysis may show to be of questionable value.[9]

The need to ensure a continued, unified policy of anti-fraud surveillance of the activities of international securities markets has become even more acute in the last decade, following the greater degree of internationalisation of capital markets. The development of a 24-hour, globalised market for internationally traded securities has led to an increase in regulatory problems caused by competing jurisdictional differences, coupled with a greater willingness on the part of financial practitioners to seek out commercial environments from which to operate whose regulatory requirements are less stringent than those imposed in their home state, a practice commonly referred to as 'regulatory arbitrage'.

The main areas of fraudulent activity which possess the greatest degree of commercial risk in the trading of securities are:

- market manipulation;
- insider dealing;
- trading of worthless securities.

Market manipulation

Market manipulation occurs wherever an individual or group operates in such a way as to bring undue influence to bear, thus affecting the value of a share. The most commonly observed illustration of such behaviour is during a contested takeover of the shares of one company by another.

When the shares of a publicly quoted company are traded on a public exchange, it would be possible, in theory, for a competing, predator company who wished to acquire the assets of its competitor in order to put it out of business or to undermine its customer base, to purchase sufficient shares of its competitor in order to obtain a controlling interest.

> As Marx noted long ago, it is a feature of competitive capitalism that the more successful enterprises which prosper drive the less successful out of business or swallow them up. The result is an increasing concentration of industry, sector by sector, in a few giant corporations, a trend to oligopoly and monopoly.[16]

The Guinness affair illustrated most clearly the techniques used by ambitious and unscrupulous practitioners to manipulate the price of the shares of two companies locked in a contested takeover battle. It was alleged that certain Guinness controllers organised what was called a share support scheme, during which they spent £25 million to underwrite friends' and business associates' purchases of Guinness shares, guaranteeing them against loss, in order to ensure that the value of Guinness shares rose in value on the stock market. The eventual outcome of the Guinness affair, during which a number of prominent business people were convicted and sentenced to terms of imprisonment, uncovered several examples of unacceptable commercial behaviour; although many financial practitioners were heard to sympathise with the plight of those convicted, on the basis that they had only been doing what so many of their friends and professional colleagues had hitherto believed was acceptable City behaviour.

Insider dealing

Insider dealing is a criminal activity which in many cases flows directly from the activities of those engaged in merger or takeover activity. Generally speaking, share prices display a tendency to rise in price after a public bid has been made for them. An investor in possession of the knowledge that a bid is about to be made for a particular stock, or indeed, in possession of any information which could directly affect the price of a particular share, is in a position to make a considerable short-term profit by buying as much of the stock as he or she can acquire prior to the announcement of the bid, and then selling once the share price has risen.

Such people are said to be trading on 'inside information' and their activities are widely prohibited by nations whose capital markets' commercial success depends upon the perception in the mind of those who trade in them that no one in the market is permitted to have an unfair advantage over other market participants. Perhaps unsurprisingly, this is a Pyrrhic perception. Insider dealing has quickly come to be appreciated not merely for its abilities to provide a major new facility to clean up dirty money, but as a profit centre in its own right. The organised criminal groups who set out deliberately to profit from concerted insider activity quickly came to pose the biggest source of concern to the London International Stock Exchange.

> This category is, in the Stock Exchange's view, the most serious. It consists of dealing rings and syndicates that have been deliberately set up to exchange items of inside information and exploit it to the maximum. Until 1986, few would admit that such rings operated in London, but it is now clear that they do. In fact, cases have come to light where such rings have constructed complex nominee networks overseas, often in the so-called 'haven' of off-shore jurisdictions . . . There is a fourth category which has not yet been clearly recognised in Britain, but which is known to exist and this is organised crime groups. For some considerable time various organised crime groups have recognised that economic crime is a high reward and low risk activity. Consequently, they have become increasingly involved in a variety of economic crimes not only to generate profit, but to maximise the return that they obtain on their investments, generated from other criminal activities; to facilitate money laundering and to achieve penetration of legitimate business activities.[17]

Trading of worthless securities

Finally, the trading of worthless securities is an activity which undermines the very basis of the market itself. Prior to the Wall Street Crash of 1929, approximately 20 million Americans took advantage of the post-war prosperity boom and tried to make a fortune on the stock market. Between 1918 and 1929, of the $50 billion worth of new securities offered to the public, half proved to be worthless.

The pedlars of worthless securities are still in business today, and their activities were most commonly observed in Great Britain during the promotion of popular capitalism through privatisation. This classic 'Thatcherite' policy was aimed at the radicalisation of the lower middle class, by encouraging them to acquire a taste for the personal possession of property, both real and intangible, leading to a reduction of their dependence on the paternalistic benevolence of the State for the supply of their services and needs and inculcating putative bourgeois habits of ownership, possession and the control of contracted services through financial independence. Supplying the ready market of willing first-time investors, who were intended to be the vanguard of the equity-owning democracy, with underpriced shares in the newly privatised industries became the publicly acceptable face of denationalisation.

Despite the best intentions of those concerned in the creation of the new investor-protection legislation however, a large sector of the British investing public became the unwilling dupes of the activities of a large number of organised criminals who flocked to London to take advantage of this new, deregulated financial market.

These companies and others like them, many of whom had close associations with US mafia-associated front men, took advertising space in newspapers and magazines offering 'commission-free dealings', and sat back and waited for the phones to ring. They did not have to wait long! Once hooked, and with their valuable allotment letters safely in the hands of the share hucksters, the luckless punters found themselves the recipients of unsolicited telephone calls from these boiler-room operations, offering them new and exotic investments in securities products of no worth, being either the subject of official restraint in the US, or of very little merit, some representing companies that did not even exist, but which they were told possessed great future financial potential.

The most significant of these operators was Thomas F Quinn,

a disbarred American securities lawyer with a long history of securities laws violations in the US and the UK who, together with a number of criminal associates, operated in London for a number of years in the 1980s. Companies with names such as Equity Management Services, Falcontrust Financial Ltd, Prudentrust Financial SA of Switzerland or Kettler Investment Finanz AG of Liechtenstein all formed part of Quinn's dishonest network of companies. Over $250 million was fraudulently taken from investors during 1987–88 alone and the subsequent investigation revealed 'a level of sophistication reminiscent of organised crime'.[18]

Increasingly, we are observing the re-emergence of an old form of investment fraud, commonly called a 'Ponzi' scheme. Named after its inventor, Charles T Ponzi, the scheme works on the basis of paying early investors out of the proceeds of the income from later investors, literally 'robbing Peter to pay Paul'. In order to survive, more and more investors must be encouraged to join the scheme to provide the money necessary to pay the dividends or interest promised to those who joined the scheme earlier. Other forms of the scheme include 'pyramid' schemes or 'chain-letters', all of which are merely variations on a theme.

In Romania, the schemes have been referred to as 'lotteries', most recently, the infamous example trading under the name of 'Caritas'. Our most recent information is that these forms of entity are now being marketed in Romania by referring to the schemes as 'insurance companies'. Using this nomenclature means that potential customers will have to examine the proposals offered to them very carefully indeed to ascertain whether the company is indeed a bona fide insurance company, underwritten by access to established insurance and re-insurance corporations, or whether it is merely a lottery or Ponzi scheme in another guise. Sadly, until the Romanians can introduce financial services style legislation to regulate such vehicles, we fear that this kind of fraud will proliferate.

Futures and derivatives fraud

The futures and derivatives industry is particularly prone to exploitation at the hands of organised crime and professional money launderers alike, and has been a willing accomplice to the dishonest movement of huge sums of hot money for many years.

As a professional's tool for the management of financial risk, the derivatives market is claimed by its practitioners to provide their institutional clients with the extra edge. As a means of assisting at least one group of their specialist clients, the professional money launderers who enable the drug trafficker, the terrorist and the organised criminal to disguise the sources of their criminal money, it certainly has no equal. Whether the derivatives market could be used to provide a subversive political group or criminally motivated country with the means to infiltrate and destabilise the structures of a Western capital market has yet to be determined. Paul Erdman's doomsday scenario in *The Panic of '89*[19] has yet to be played out in full, but any volatile financal product which has the potential to provide such a high degree of instability to international financial markets has the potential to be used as an 'offensive weapon' by such groups and must therefore be considered with an informed mind.

These are still early days and many of the new risk-management products presently being designed sail in very uncharted financial waters, but their proponents are already only too anxious to talk down their inherent risk factors in an attempt to head off any introduction of a greater degree of regulation which would adversely affect their ability to make short-term profits. The existence of the 'greed' factor as a means of determining an integral component of the white collar criminal process should never be underestimated. [20]

However, before discussing their criminal use, in order to understand the risks posed by these esoteric markets and products it is first necessary to understand their legitimate use. It is no part of the authors' brief to provide a detailed description of the historical development of the derivatives market, but it is necessary to be able to place the rapid development of the scope and use of the derivatives market in perspective.

In a joint SEC/CFTC report published in December 1982 the authors noted:

Many institutions are still at the stage of sampling the new financial product markets to get a 'feel' for them. Several institutions reported that the availability of index options and futures, particularly as they become more accepted by institutional investors, may actually increase their overall commitment of capital to the equities markets. These products provide an efficient means to reduce market exposure, and their flexibility allows institutions to pursue investment strategies not possible or economic in their absence.[21]

The primary use of derivatives was to manage and reduce financial risk. Traditionally they were a professional's tool, used to earn incremental returns on managed money, allocate assets to adjust for market risk, or manage various commercial or financial risks, including interest rate and exchange rate risks. In effect, derivatives products made it possible to fix the price at which an asset could be bought or sold in the future, or the interest rate at which money could be borrowed or lent. A derivatives position could be established whose market value tended to vary inversely with the price or interest rate exposure that was being hedged. Thus losses on a cash position that resulted from the movement of prices or interest rates could be offset by the gains obtained from the derivatives position.

This now 'traditional' perception of the use of derivatives represented the thinking current in the early days of the development of the market. However, the growing willingness to introduce a greater degree of deregulation into financial markets, the increasing level of constructive innovation capable of being generated by developments in communications technology and the globalisation of financial markets mean that in the last ten years, derivatives markets have undergone a dramatic change in both the products they trade and the way in which they are traded.

These trends include the dramatic rise in floating rate financing opportunities; massive securitization of mortgages and other financial products; sweeping internationalization of the trading of currencies, bonds and equities; a striking shift towards institutionalization of portfolio investment; and a worldwide explosion of budgetary deficits and the associated mushrooming of so-called risk-free government bonds, which provide ample raw material for many advanced derivatives strategies.[22]

It is important to emphasise that the risks the professional hedgers seek to avoid are not created by the derivative markets themselves, but are inherent in the hedger's underlying commercial or financial activities. However, in many if not most cases, the party on the other side of the hedger's contract is a speculator who adopts the risk exposure in the hope of profiting thereby.

It is this aspect of the trading involvement of the speculator which adds greatly to the volume of transactions in derivatives markets, thus increasing the liquidity of the market. Increased liquidity makes it easier for those wishing to hedge to establish and quickly close out positions in the market, while enabling greater efficiency to be maintained in both cash and derivatives markets by various forms of arbitrage trading, whereby the trader takes a position in the derivatives market and an equal opposite position in the underlying cash market, in the hope of achieving a profit by exploiting the differential between the two. Nevertheless, the involvement of the speculator in the derivatives market introduces an important psychological element which tends to be reflected within the market sector generally and goes some way to explain one of the most inherently dangerous risk factors.

As a medium for fraud, the futures market provides particularly valuable facilities. Any floor trader or 'local' trader on the floor of a futures exchange is in an almost unique position to conduct a dishonest trade or launder 'funny' money, particularly when trading together with a friend or counterparty trader and front-running a series of transactions for his or her own account. Locals trade on their own account; they are liable for their debts and they must meet their obligations to the floor. Black money can be cleared through their trading account and used to settle 'hedged' losses, while the profits can be paid out of clean money, the local being paid a hefty commission.

A number of well-known London commodity trading houses offered exchange control evasion facilities in the late 1970s, one operating its own 'ghost' office in Bahrain to create fictitious Arab clients who wished to trade commodity futures on London markets. The monies subsequently transferred to accounts in

Zug or Liechtenstein, when the accounts were closed and the relevant export certificates obtained from the Bank of England, belonged instead to wealthy British tax evaders who were willing to pay up to 10 per cent of the capital moved for the privilege.

Another London broker was arrested in 1984, after information was supplied by the FBI in San Francisco that he was creating fictitious US tax losses by laundering $1 million a month through his company, as part of a complex 'year-end tax-straddle' arrangement. He listened with amazement while the detectives interviewing him suggested that he might have been knowingly moving Mafia money. He had no doubts, he assured them glibly, that such was the case. He was not paid to make moral judgements about the source of the money he introduced to the company, as in his world there was no such thing as clean money or dirty money, there was only money!

A German commodities fraudster operating out of London and the Isle of Man attempted to purchase all the seats on the New Orleans Commodities Exchange in order to be able to control his own personal futures exchange, with the intention of disguising the huge sums of money being obtained by his counterparts who were operating other fraudulent futures trading companies in London. Such an ambition is not as far-fetched as it might at first appear.

A major investigation by the FBI culminated in 1989 with the uncovering of a multi-million dollar fraud and money-laundering operation run by an organised crime syndicate on the floor of Chicago's prestigious futures exchanges, the Chicago Board of Trade and the Chicago Mercantile Exchange. 'Federal investigators were tipped off to the money laundering scheme by street informants, while the enquiry into cheating on the exchange floors was begun after individuals within the futures industry itself asked the FBI for help in rooting out fraud.'[23]

The French Futures Supervisory Council recognised in 1990 that their exchange, the MATIF, was wide open to abuse by money launderers. They responded by requiring each exchange member to nominate one member to maintain permanent contact with the Council and with the Finance Ministry unit which monitors all suspicious financial market operations.

The activities of Capcom Commodities, one of the London-based, BCCI-related institutions, gave a unique insight to US investigators looking into the use of the futures markets for laundering dirty money. The words of the US Customs Chief in charge of the BCCI-related 'Operation 'C' Chase', William van Raab, were not merely idle comment when he said, 'One thing we learned from this investigation is that the Colombian narcotics traffickers see Europe as a fantastic opportunity for two reasons. First, they can sell coke for twice the price they get in the United States. And second, for the wide-open financial institutions that exist there.'[24]

Those 'wide-open' institutions are typified by the futures and derivatives markets which pose a particular risk, not only because of the 'anonymous' nature of their trading strategies – all brokers trade as principals – but also because of their increased use by other investment institutions for complex hedging and risk-spreading strategies when traded in conjunction with stock baskets and indices; the increased use of 'designer' derivatives, some of which are so complicated they can only exist as theoretical mathematical models, for non-hedging, wholly speculative purposes; and on their own as trading strategies, particularly in the form of off-shore traded funds. Trading futures and derivatives speculatively is what is known as a 'zero sum' game, for every winner there has to be a loser. As both paper profits and paper losses can be used as a means of concealing money flows, these techniques have no equal, even in well-regulated markets, which makes them such an attractive medium for the fraudster and the 'funny money' men who are looking all the time for new means to steal from their clients and to disguise money. The more volatile or risk-based the trading product, the greater the degree of movement and therefore, the greater the degree of potential profit or loss.

The very real danger for those who administer the derivatives markets is that the techniques which underpin their function as efficient risk- management facilities make them so attractive to criminal elements who wish to use them for dishonest purposes. At the same time, the markets must constantly attract considerable amounts of capital in order to generate the high degree of liquidity they require to function effectively, which is why they will always offer a warm welcome to high net-worth individuals whatever the source of their money. Thus their function must and will increasingly become the target for investigative oversight.

It is not hard to understand why the most vociferous apologists for egregious misconduct which periodically surfaces in these highly volatile markets, and the biggest opponents of increased regulatory control, are the professional practitioners themselves who are only too well aware that the enormous degree of profitability presently being realised depends to a great degree on the absence of regulatory controls.[25]

Free-market sentiments, while no doubt espousing all the traditional values of the *laissez-faire* approach to market regulation, fail to acknowledge the impact of the far greater degree of globalisation of capital markets which has taken place in the last ten years. This factor has led to Alan Greenspan, the Chairman of the US Federal Reserve, warning bankers of the dangers that derivatives instruments could cause to financial markets; and how the immediate effects of the discovery of financial misjudgement in one global sector would be felt as secondary financial disruption very much faster in another time zone. [26] Those who were responsible for BCCI recognised the real worth of the derivatives markets as a means of laundering cash and assets, so much so that they made considerable use of a derivatives trading company called Capcom Financial Services Ltd, run by Syed Akbar, a former BCCI Treasury official, to facilitate their dishonest aims.[27]

Non-hedging, derivatives speculation is literally no different from gambling on horse races or games of chance, and its practitioners tend to possess the same commercial mentality as the gambler. Many of those private clients who engage in such speculative practices, such as the large number of wealthy Islamic speculators who have been increasingly drawn to the derivatives markets, do so because the markets contain the very gambling element which would be denied them by strict religious observance, but which enables them to indulge in a favourite vice by justifying it on the basis that it is a commercial trading facility which does not fall within the definition of the prohibited practices. On the other hand, the professional speculators or 'locals' who own or rent 'seats' on the floor of the exchange at their own financial risk are little different from professional gamblers.

In all cases they are playing with their own money, although some are also employed to facilitate strategic position taking by other professional practitioners.

At the same time, both floor and desk market professionals tend to be heavily influenced by a trading culture which preaches the virtues of adopting a grossed-out, high-profiled, aggressive, risk-taking personality, which needs to be constantly attested to. Michael Lewis, who coined the phrase 'big swinging dick' to define this macho mentality in his seminal work *Liar's Poker*,[28] describes the behaviour of the traders on one specialist derivatives desk at Salomon Brothers, who profitably traded one of the most mathematically complex derivatives products:

> The money was made with ever more refined tools of analysis. But the traders did not become correspondingly more refined in their behaviour. For each step forward in market technology they took a step backward in human evolution . . . Each Friday was 'food frenzy' day, during which all trading ceased and eating commenced . . . A customer would call in and ask us to bid or offer bonds and you'd have to say, 'I'm sorry but we're in the middle of the feeding frenzy, I'll call you back.'

Five years on, very little has changed. Jeremy Warner, the City Editor of the *Independent on Sunday*, describes the present situation:

> The first thing you notice about a Swiss Bank derivatives man is that generally speaking he doesn't wear a suit (except when he's giving the client a hard sell). It's all blue jeans and open-neck shirts, even the occasional pony tail and ear-ring ... it sticks out like a sore thumb in the City's stuffed shirt environment.[29]

Psychologically, these men and women are regulatorily resistant. Theirs is a primarily deviant, norm-evasive, criminogenic culture, not much given to the willing acceptance of regulatory control.[30] These are the traders to whom the compliance officer is generally seen as 'the business prevention officer', and the traders tend to view each new regulatory notice as an irritating inconvenience standing in the way of increasingly innovative trading. Each new regulatory requirement is looked upon as a challenge to the ingenuity of the traders, and competitions are held by dealers to see who can get round the controls undiscovered, and in the most criminally profitable manner.[31]

In October 1992, a former Commodity Futures Trading Commission executive director and the manager of a Swiss brokerage firm were sentenced to imprisonment in New York for bank fraud involving over $1 million worth of counterfeit securities and for laundering the proceeds. As part of the laundering process, they opened brokerage accounts at the Swiss company to disguise the movement of the money, which they obtained by fraudulently cashing counterfeit cheques obtained in the US in Switzerland and the United Arab Emirates.

BCCI's Treasury Division 'lost' £633 million under the control of Syed Ziauddin Ali Akbar, who was also described as the creative force behind its otherwise flourishing commodity broking operation, Capcom. Akbar resigned from Capcom in October 1988 when he was arrested and charged with laundering narcotics money while at BCCI, for which he was subsequently convicted and served a prison sentence.

Managed off-shore funds

It is in the related field of off-shore futures funds and other managed funds that one of the biggest risks to investors and financial institutions from fraud and 'funny money' is posed, because of the inherently volatile nature of futures-related products; the lack of access to hard information audit trails if things go wrong; and the very nature of the product itself. Off-shore futures funds are rated AAA in the 'ask me no questions – I'll tell you no lies' school of financial skulduggery, and yet their use as an investment medium is growing dramatically. Off-shore investment funds generally fell into disrepute in the late 1960s with the demise of capital flight guru Bernie Cornfeld's Investors Overseas Services (IOS), but in the 1990s they are back in business.

Mutual funds, hedge funds, insurance companies, banks and brokerage firms have all piled into the game, whether as sponsors or as investment advisers chosen by U.S. or non-U.S. sponsors. Fund-of-funds and manager-of-managers arrangements have proliferated ... Overseas firms have been acquired, wholly or in part, by U.S. institutions, and these have in turn, registered funds offshore. The organization of many offshore funds is so complex that it sometimes takes considerable sleuthing to ferret out sponsorship, administrative and management relationships.[32]

Those who manage and promote these funds claim that they are now highly organised and squeaky clean, but many fund officials still recognise that drug money is attracted to their products for laundering. 'An offshore fund is nothing more than a currency transfer centre' says one official of a New York based offshore fund group.[33]

The markets and the products they trade have developed and expanded considerably in the last five years. Much of the stimulus for this development has been provided by economic and financial conditions which have made it possible for new derivative products to be created, developed and marketed. Henry Kaufman identifies six factors which have facilitated the rapid growth in derivatives products: the reduction in world inflation; the emergence of what Kaufman calls a 'steep, positively sloped, yield curve'; the increase in access to capital market activities; the emergence of large pools of risk capital under the control of aggressive fund managers; sudden outbursts of unusual price volatility in specific financial markets (such as during the ERM crisis in Europe when off-shore hedge fund operators sold the British Pound so aggressively that Britain was forced to withdraw from the ERM); and finally, the development of a parallel market in relatively cheap, accessible, computerised technology which enables the complex mathematical calculations necessary to realise the maximum profitability from extended exposure in swaps and options.[34]

Drawing on Kaufman's analysis, which posits a market-oriented perspective, and supported by other sources of information and intelligence, it becomes possible to provide an alternative analysis which possesses a greater capability of providing a more realistic risk/threat assessment of the dangers inherent in the increasingly unregulated use of the derivatives market.

The reduction in world inflation observed by Kaufman to be

an encouragement to invest in financial assets, the emergence of the steep yield curve, the increased access to capital markets and the emergence of large pools of risk capital, have all been influenced, at least in part, by a sustained reduction in interest rates in mature capitalist economies, which, coupled with the greater availability of globalised traded instruments, has led to a greater willingness for owners of available capital to look elsewhere for more entrepreneurial means of achieving growth in invested funds. Add to this the huge slush-funds of surplus capital, in the form of bank deposits vastly in excess of withdrawals, which have been sloshing around in many US and European financial institutions based in cities most closely associated with traditional, narcotics cross-border entry points, and the picture of the type of capital available for investment begins to take on a different perspective.

Off-shore funds do not necessarily have to be sited in exotic Caribbean locations, however, in order to pose a huge degree of risk as a laundering medium to professionals and advisers. The development of a tariff-barrier-free Europe has meant that financial institutions have been enabled to move freely within the Union and allowed to create investment product services in one country which can be marketed in all the other countries within the EU. The directive to allow cross-border selling of mutual funds, investment trusts, unit trusts and collective investment instruments among member states without requiring those funds to register in each individual state is known as the Undertaking for Collective Investment in Transferable Securities, or UCITS for short. Putting it at its simplest, the directive represents a charter for the money launderers.

The UCITS 'theory' states that the structure of the investment product itself need only comply with the rules of the EC member state in which it is created. Again, in theory, all member states now conform to a unified standard of financial compliance in the creation of financial products, the well-known 'level playing field' standard. It is only when the product is marketed in another state that the internal marketing rules of that individual state apply. The question that practitioners need to ask themselves therefore, if European regulatory standards really are considered to possess the necessary degree of equivalency, is why so many of these funds are based in Luxembourg? Could it perhaps have something to do with that country's notoriously strict banking secrecy regulations and its reputation as a tax and investment haven? If the point has not been made, it is worth recalling that Luxembourg was one of the two jurisdictions of choice for Agha Hasan Abedi when first registering his banking interests in BCCI.

The directive allows US funds registered in Europe to enjoy the same privileges as those possessed by EU members. It may come as very little surprise to discover that almost as soon as the directive had been passed a deluge of international fund advisers, banks and investment houses flooded in to register their interests. 'The rush to register in the Grand Duchy was so frenetic, beginning in early 1990 that you couldn't get a fund launched without significant delay.'[35]

One of the main attractions to US financial institutions in the setting up of independently registered companies in the 'offshore' environment is that they have been able to circumvent many of the administrative regulations imposed upon them at home regarding the identities of clients or account holders, position limits and reporting requirements. These regulations have been created to protect the US markets from over-exposure to uncovered risk incurred by speculators, and to limit market manipulation by individuals or groups acting in concert. They also provide for complex audit provisions to enable trading to be analysed and constantly monitored. Allowing them to be circumvented by the creation of off-shore entities is an open invitation to organised crime to gain yet another foothold in the control process, but the promoters of both futures and investment funds can still circumvent all the provisions designed to protect the integrity of US capital markets by the simple expedient of registering in one of the 'funny money' havens.

> The registration process is now routine and has proved to be an efficient way to get products into overseas markets. Funds don't have to endure the tedious regulatory scrutiny of the Securities and Exchange Commission; once the paperwork is completed, a new fund effectively can be registered in the Cayman Islands, the Bahamas or the British Virgin Islands in three days.[36]

Insurance fraud

The concept of insurance, the ability to provide oneself with financial protection against potential future loss or damage, is an integral part of all free-market commercial practice. Individuals can insure themselves against death, serious injury, chronic illness, fire, flood, theft, loss and damage to their property. Most financial enterprises, particularly those involving the lending of money against some form of fixed security or the delivery of valuable commodities, require some form of insurance policy to be taken out to cover the financial interests of the lender or the end-user, in the event of loss or damage to the security for the loan or the deliverable commodity. Major companies can insure themselves against the loss of an important director or executive, while famous public performers can insure those attributes, such as their voice, which provide their means of earning a living. The American film actress Betty Grable was reputed to have insured her legs for $1 million.

To some extent, the provision of insurance cover is a form of gambling. The providers of the cover are 'betting' against themselves that they will not have to pay out the cover requested, and indeed, in many cases of insured cover, the insured loss does not occur and the providers are not called upon to pay up. It can be seen immediately how attractive insurance companies could be to a fraudster, and indeed, for many years, fraudulent insurance companies flourished in the UK and the US, until stringent regulation brought the provision of their service and function into line.

The person taking out the insurance cover pays a 'premium' to the provider of the cover, the amount of 'premium' required being proportional to the level of risk which the insurer believes is being covered. The skill involved in the calculation of the premium to be paid is considerable, and the insurer therefore requires a complete disclosure of all the known risks involved in the transaction, before it is possible to reach an accurate financial calculation. A failure to make full and frank disclosure can result in the cover being rendered void.

It is not difficult to appreciate that insurance is very big business indeed, generating considerable revenue flows and, because it relies to a great extent on the word of the insured that he or she has suffered the requisite degree of claimable loss, is an industry which has traditionally experienced a high degree of fraudulent activity. There is a tendency among many individuals, even those who might not otherwise exhibit criminogenic potential, to view the insurance company as 'fair game' when it comes to the making of a false or inflated claim. The making of such false claims, however, increases the level of uncalculated loss which the insurance company is required to pay, thus reducing its profitability. In a highly competitive commercial market, reduced profitability leads to loss of financial confidence among investors. Thus insurance fraud tends to create a vicious circle of ever-increasing demands by the insurers for higher premiums, to offset fraudulent losses; increased disclosure requirements to ensure that all the relevant facts are known prior to cover being granted; and a greater degree of post-loss investigation, in the event of a claim. These aspects, in their turn, have a tendency to alienate potential customers, who resent the implication that the business they wish to undertake with the insurance company is the kind that requires additional surveillance.

The competitiveness of the insurance market is such, however, that, rather than attract a reputation for being too unsympathetic to client claims, the companies will pay out those claims which they know may be made by professional fraudsters, but which will be pursued vigorously by the claimants. This is because they know that their alternative is to defend an action by the insured in the civil court, with the high burden of proof required to prove fraud, and the commensurate likelihood of bad or adverse publicity if they fail. At the same time they make smaller but honest claims difficult to pursue, in the hope that the honest but more unsophisticated claimant will eventually get tired of the remorseless bureaucracy being demanded, and abandon the claim.

The insurance industry, because of the immediacy of its impact upon all sectors of the community, plays one of the most important roles in facilitating institutional cash-flow within the wider investment market. Premium income from the sale of policies is itself used to invest in other forms of revenue-producing products. In those countries where the investing public may not possess a high degree of financial sophistication and would be less likely to undertake direct investment in securities or other forms of directly marketed investments, access to insurance-based investment products to encourage a free flow of investment capital is of paramount importance. As a means of stimulating investment in these instruments, governments have often provided generous tax treatments for premiums invested in such financial vehicles. The principles which underpin these investment products are the need for the investment company to be able to guarantee continued retention of investor's capital for as long a period of time as possible. To ensure this result, the investment policies are constructed in a way which provides for punitive treatment of early encashment by the investor, and for a 'bonus' to be paid at the very end of the investment life of the product. The longer the investment is left with the institution, the larger the terminal bonus offered.

The selling of such products and the sales techniques used by the investment companies have become a significant cause for concern in recent years in the UK, because of the huge propensity for fraud on the part of those who are responsible for the marketing of such products. It is now widely perceived that without stringent investor protection provisions, the level of fraudulent conduct within these markets will lead to an undermining of public confidence in the market itself, leading to a loss of financial legitimacy. Such a perception is not widely shared by the industry itself, which finds its own best financial interests served by the continued turnover of investment-type products on a regular basis.

Salespeople, by the way in which they are paid, have been tacitly encouraged to indulge in the widespread mis-selling of financial policies, otherwise known as 'churning', in order both to enhance their own commission income, and to ensure a regular cash-flow of new capital. Such wholesale and uncompromising allegations are strongly resented by the life and pensions industry, which spends a considerable amount of money on public relations consultants, image manipulators and 'spin' doctors, in an attempt to maintain in the mind of the public the perception of their high standards and probity. However, the indisputable facts of industrial malpractice and the levels of disciplinary intervention being undertaken by the regulators speak too eloquently for themselves. When the lead regulator of the British financial market can openly acknowledge the institutionalised mis-selling of pension policies to literally hundreds of thousands of gullible financial unsophisticates, it does not behove us to take industry protestations of honour and commercial integrity too seriously.

Fraud in international trade

Ever since humans first learned how to sail beyond the sight of their own coastline, and returned home with strange and wonderful souvenirs of their travels, international markets have developed to provide the means to enable producing countries and consuming countries to trade with one another to their mutual benefit. For many developing countries, the money they are able to earn from the sale of their raw materials on world markets is the only means they have of ensuring an inflow of hard Western currency. Dishonest practices, such as the shipping of adulterated products, the fraudulent sale of non-existent goods or the theft of the goods in transit, pose a considerable risk to their economies. Any valuable commodity which can be shipped or transported becomes the target for the fraudster and the international criminal; valuable products such as drugs, complex mechanical component parts or expensive luxury items can be counterfeited and substituted for the real product, while valuable products can be contaminated by extortionists demanding blackmail payments.

In recent years, one classic example has been the proliferation of Nigerian oil frauds. Oil is an internationally traded commodity with an army of buyers and intermediaries ready and willing to make a market in spot oil cargoes. The Nigerian scams have been perpetrated by fraudsters making use of forged documents who offer to sell parcels of high-quality crude to willing but unsuspecting buyers. In many cases, the forged documents are related to consignments of oil already in transit on the seas, being carried in identifiable ships in confirmable quantities. The fraudsters give the date of delivery of the oil and its unloading port and ask the purchaser to open a letter of credit for the full value of the cargo, but at the same time request an advance payment

of, say, $300,000 in a Swiss Bank as soon as the sale confir-
mation documents issued by the Nigerian National Petroleum
Commission (NNPC) have been received and the ships' master
has confirmed that the consignment has been lifted. The NNPC
documents, which would be forgeries, would be quickly received
by the putative purchasers, while the ship's master would respond
positively to a telex requesting confirmation of lifting. Having
paid the $300,000, the purchasers would wait for the arrival of
the ship, only to find that the load which they thought was theirs
belonged, in fact, to another purchaser with a prior claim.

Many variations of such frauds have been discovered, in all
too many cases, when the fraudsters have made off with the
money and are beyond discovery. The NNPC have themselves
been the victim of a number of oil frauds, involving the advance
lifting of large amounts of crude by fraudulent prospectors
claiming to be drilling for oil in the Nigerian oilfields; the cargoes
have been immediately sold on the spot market while the fraudsters have quietly abandoned their 'prospecting' efforts.

Another problem which has caused increasing concern to international regulators and legislators has been the growth of
hijacking and the piracy relating to ships at sea, both in the form
of the boarding of the ships themselves and killing the master
and crew before sailing the ship into a safe harbour from where
the cargo is unloaded; or the more sophisticated frauds of cargo
deviation or even the phantom ship phenomenon. The deviation
method was particularly prevalent in the Eastern Mediterranean
where the owners of ageing, low-value ships would offer their
vessels for freighting, but with no intention of delivering the cargo
to its intended destination. The low freight rates being asked are
very attractive to traders who perceive an enhanced profit margin
thereby, and the owners have had little difficulty in filling their
ships with cargoes which are often worth more than the ship
itself. Once loaded and on the high seas, the ship deviates from
its plotted course and sails to the Lebanon, which during the
height of the Lebanese civil war put it beyond the reach of any
international jurisdiction. The cargoes are broken up and sold
and the ship is then able to be re-named and re-flagged. In some
cases, evidence has been received of false reports of the ship
having sunk.

The concept of the 'phantom' ship fraud has been particular prevalent in the Far East where very powerful criminal groups, with access to corrupt employees within the national ship registries of such countries as Panama and Honduras, have created wholly false registrations for ships which, having been chartered to load high-value cargoes, simply disappear with their consignments, only to reappear again later under another name or in another guise.

Product counterfeiting is probably one of the most valuable international trade frauds. It is very difficult to place any kind of realistic figure on the volume of counterfeit or 'snide' products curently in existence – in these areas all figures tend to be 'soft' – but estimates by informed US Government Trade Commissions have placed the figure as high as 6 per cent of total world trade. Brand name products maintain their valuable market share because of the strictnesss of the quality control which they employ in the finishing of their product. Cheaper, less stringently produced products, manufactured to lower tolerance levels, as in the case of counterfeit aircraft parts, or lower chemical standards, as in the case of bogus pharmaceuticals, pose real threats to the safety of the end-users. In addiition no one is going to underestimate the dangers to societies from the sale of blood for transfusion purposes which has been obtained without having been properly screened for the HIV virus.

Tax evasion and the misuse of tax havens

In this world nothing can be said to be certain, except death and taxes.
Benjamin Franklin, 1789

Chiselled into the granite portico of the Internal Revenue Service's building in Washington, DC are the words: 'Taxes are what we pay to live in a free society'. Such egalitarian sentiments may well have reflected the original *raison d'être* for the raising of direct taxation from the citizens of the state, but as time has passed, the imposition of taxation has become used as much as a means of providing a political means of social and economic control, as the mere raising of revenue.

The use after the Second World War of structured taxation levels to achieve a more equitable redistribution of wealth created considerable resentment among those upon whom the greatest taxation burden fell, leading to an increased greater perception of fiscal unfairness and the reduction of incentive to create wealth. This situation contributed another facet to the capitalist paradox, as those with the greatest need to protect their wealth from the grasp of acquisitive chancellors were also those with sufficient means to pay for the expensive advice available to enable them to avoid paying any more tax than was absolutely necessary, and to minimise such taxes to which they were already subject. This ensured that, in practice, they paid proportionally less in tax than the poorer members of society. The dichotomy thus expressed in the moral conundrum of the difference between lawful tax avoidance, generally perceived to be the legitimate work-product of the bona fide tax adviser, and criminal tax evasion, the illegitimate activities of those who seek to hide their lawfully taxable proceeds from the fiscal authorities, has been reflected in the competing effectiveness of tax shelters as opposed to tax havens.

Tax shelters

Tax shelters are invariably the physical manifestation of informed legal analysis of existing fiscal legislation, expressed in tangible form. Their primary function is to provide a legal form of tax avoidance, expressed, most usually, in the provision of a medium for the creation of a tax-saving incentive for high-net-worth individuals by encouraging them to invest in theoretically socially responsible activities, or in methods which might not otherwise attract such a high rate of investment. Their attraction to wealthy individuals in the United States in the 1980s as a means of sheltering tax burdens caused a proliferation of companies dealing in such facilities as commodity futures speculation, which through the use of 'year-end tax straddles' enabled extensive tax write-offs to take place; while the leasing of energy-saving equipment, coupled with the generation of alternative forms of non-fossil fuel sources of energy creation, encouraged the development of tax-shelter schemes of quite breath-taking audacity.

Tax shelters were, however, inevitably a high-cost operation, involving the use of expensive lawyers and accountants. Because they were designed to be declared to the revenue authorities, they were constantly under review and subject to reform. The possibility always existed that a tax-saving device could be created, sometimes at considerable cost to the end-user, only to be later overturned by an unsympathetic court judgement, or outlawed by subsequent changes in the law. The inevitable effect of reduced opportunities for sheltered revenue led inexorably to greater recourse to the use of tax havens and thus an institutionalised level of tax evasion.

Tax havens

Tax havens are sovereign 'off-shore' countries with an advanced degree of willingness to permit foreign, non-resident, high-rate tax payers to deposit funds secretly, to hide behind anonymous corporate fronts, or to form highly complex trust arrangements. They exist for the simple reason that, as long as they do not provide too many barriers to the inflow of cash, enormous sums of money will continue to flow into their jurisdiction, and remain safe from the prying eyes of the fiscal authorities of the country of origin. Such facilities, while being legal within the haven state itself, place high-net-worth individuals who have recourse to their services in very considerable difficulties in their home jurisdiction if the revenue authorities discover that they are making use of evasion vehicles. For this reason, an obsessive level of secrecy and the guarantee of complete discretion in the handling of the client's affairs, are the hallmarks of the most successful tax havens.

The use of such facilities is not necessarily a contemporary phenomenon. Meyer Lansky, the leading Mafia money launderer, is reported to have been making his first forays into European off-shore banking as far back as 1932, setting up a Swiss bank account to hide the profits of Governor Huey Long of Louisiana, who had allowed Lansky and his associates to open up slot-machine houses in New Orleans. The use of the Swiss facilities introduced Lansky to the enormous range of banking and financial services which the Swiss were prepared to offer, which he would use and develop in later years, moving money from Mafia-controlled banks in Miami via the Bahamas and thus opening the door for the Sicilian Mafia to gain its terminal stranglehold on the world heroin trade.

Throughout the 1930s Lansky continued to develop his financial expertise, first in Louisiana and Florida and later in 1938 in Cuba. It was in Cuba that Lansky first became aware of the facilities available to discreet investors and tax evaders a few hundred miles away in the Bahamas, the islands to which he would later move his centre of financial operations from Cuba, following the overthrow of Batista in 1959.[37]

Such 'off-shore' secrecy facilities have been one of the main influences on the proliferation of channels for the movement of criminally generated money, whether it be in the from of the proceeds of drugs, crime or for terrorist purposes. Their purported use for 'tax' reasons however has enabled them to assume a degree of quasi-respectability which would otherwise be denied them, if the use to which they are most commonly put was openly recognised. The existence of the commercially acceptable fiction of tax avoidance as opposed to institutionalised tax evasion is another integral facet of the capitalist paradox, a fact which in itself leads directly to yet another aspect of economic crime, the laundering of dirty money.

Money laundering

Money laundering is now an extremely lucrative criminal enterprise in its own right. The Treasury's investigations have uncovered members of an emerging criminal class – professional money launderers who aid and abet other criminals through financial activities. These individuals hardly fit the stereotype of an underworld criminal. They are accountants, attorneys, money brokers and members of other legitimate professions. They need not become involved with the underlying criminal activity except to conceal and transfer the proceeds that result from it. They are drawn to their illicit activity for the same reason that drug trafficking attracts new criminals to replace those who are convicted and imprisoned – greed. Money laundering, for them, is an easy route to almost limitless wealth. [38]

The new offences of money laundering created by European member states in compliance with the European Directive on Money Laundering include within their definition money obtained through drug trafficking and through the proceeds of other criminal conduct, including money associated with terrorist activities. In an attempt to place their contribution to the laundering phenomenon in perspective, it is inevitable that we must spend a little time examining the interface between organised crime, drug trafficking and terrorism. Before we can begin to isolate and dissect specific illustrations, however, it is necessary to assert the logical indivisibility of each sector of this 'unholy trinity' in the money-laundering environment and to recognise the part that each plays in the support of the other's mutual aims and objectives.

Today, when we consider the criminological aspects of money laundering, it is not possible to make any meaningful distinction between the concepts of 'organised crime' and 'terrorism' except for necessarily imprecise journalistic reasons, and drug trafficking has long been a natural source of financing for both phenomena. Sadly, within the financial sector there has never been any well-disseminated level of understanding of the true scope of the criminal problem posed by the international trafficking in narcotics. This is due in part to the cultural unwillingness of the industry to confront the distasteful reality of the source of so much of the money they handle; and in part, to the apparent 'inability' of financiers to perceive any inchoate problem in anything other than financial terms. Therefore, in order to reinforce the degree of seriousness with which European governments view the requirements they have imposed in the new legislation, and in an attempt to define the scope of the problem which the money from such sources can pose to bankers and financial institutions, the economics of the narcotics industry become required reading. This will be dealt with in greater detail later in this Part, but the money laundering phenomenon itself, growing directly out of its tax-evasion component, must be viewed independently.

Like most social, let alone economic evils, money laundering is nothing new. It is as old as is the need to hide one's wealth from prying eyes and jealous hands, and concern about the uses and misuses of hidden money is not just an issue in our century. Of course, the modern money launderer will no doubt adopt rather more sophisticated techniques than the gem carriers of India or the Knights Templar, but his objectives and essential modus operandi will be the same. The objectives will be to obscure the source and thus, the nature of the wealth in question and the modus operandi will inevitably involve resort to transactions, real or imagined, which will be designed to confuse the onlooker and confound the enquirer.[39]

Money laundering is nothing more than an egregious use of the world's banking system, and is a truly international phenomenon. In one sense, the existence of the professional money launderer proves the fiscal effectiveness of the international banking system, because if it did not work so well, he would be less likely to be so successful. The ease with which money can be moved around the world at the flick of a switch has been facilitated by the revolution in banking which has accompanied the development of 24-hour trading. While the commercial sector has been profitably encouraged to develop new and innovative financial products, and as the world's financial markets have become more sophisticated, so the means to facilitate the transmission of money have been required to keep pace with those changes. Much of that impetus has been supplied by the technical advances made in the computer and communications industry. As technology has advanced, so new methods of laundering 'funny money' have become possible, but the laws which existed to prevent those markets and facilities from being abused by international organised crime have barely kept pace. The continued failure to recognise the importance of effective anti-money laundering legislation has led to a new and very frightening criminal environment being allowed to develop in Western Europe.

The strategy of criminal organizations is to manipulate their illicit proceeds, usually, but not always, through the legitimate financial sector, in such a manner as to make those proceeds appear to have come from a legitimate source. Thus money laundering is a vital component of all financially motivated crime. More importantly for the international community, since obfuscating any evidentiary paper or money trail is a precondition to successful money laundering, such activity will invariably involve transborder operations, often including many border crossings in the course of a laundering transaction.[40]

In our identification of the capitalist paradox, we have already illustrated how difficult it can be to differentiate between legitimate entrepreneurial commercial activity and the business activities of organised crime. At times of dynamic commercial expansion in any business sector, organised criminal enterprises compete with legitimate companies for their lucrative market share.

The new markets for European and American technology and consumer durables which are rapidly developing in the former Iron Curtain countries are no exception, as the concept of free-market enterprise pours in to fill the vacuum created by years of rigid communist dogma and planned economies. At the same time, a large number of commercially attractive but wholly fraudulent schemes are being promoted by a new generation of East European criminals, who need no lessons in deviousness from their Western counterparts and who are taking every advantage of the new atmosphere of enterprise. Many of these schemes are being openly promoted in the West, and Western bankers and other professionals are being wooed by criminal entrepreneurs who are anxious to obtain Western support and assistance to perpetrate their frauds.

In the immediate aftermath of the demise of the German Democratic Republic, those best placed to take the greatest advantage of the social chaos which had been generated by the new spirit of democracy were the very senior government officials and members of the Secret Police (Stasi) who had been responsible for imposing the former East German state's repressive regime. One £170 million fraud reported in 1990 arose from a loophole in the currency union agreement between East and West Germany, which enabled three former Stasi officers to claim preferential exchange rates for non-existent export contracts.[41]

By April 1991 former Eastern bloc countries were reporting their concerns regarding the use of their newly developing independent banking systems for money laundering. The Estonian central bank governor was to report the inflow of 'enormous amounts of foreign cash being deposited' in his country's banks in the days immediately following the creation of its own currency.[42] His expressions of concern reflected those made by the Financial Action Task Force (FATF) on money laundering at their meeting in Italy in July 1992, where it was recognised that the East European banking systems would become more attractive to the launderers as their indigenous currencies became more convertible and Western systems of banking surveillance tightened. FATF recognised that the less-developed Eastern European countries and most of the former Soviet republics presented the greatest challenge because their need for hard currency was so urgent.

The European Community is only now beginning to appreciate the unpalatable fact, which Europe's drug squad officers have long recognised, that the dream of a European barrier-free trading market, 'no money changing; no fancy transactions; no hassle',[43] will, without the most stringent financial regulatory controls, turn into a narcotics nightmare. Organised criminals need to expand their operations simply to survive. They have been so successful in 'narcotising' the US that some commentators report they have virtually saturated the available market, and they have made so much money from their activities that they are in real danger of running out of facilities with which to launder their profits. Europe represents for them the new frontier for both drug trafficking and for money laundering.

The risks to professional criminals from being engaged in money laundering can, however, be circumvented if the criminals themselves own the means of moving the money. Why run even the minimal risk of being reported to the authorities when, with a bit of ingenuity, you can create your own banking facilities?

Underground banking

As we pointed out earlier, a barrier-free Europe now stands in more danger from the threat of organised crime than at any time in its history. As the legitimate market develops, so the 'crime enterprises' in the illegitimate market, its *alter ego*, will develop with it. The phrase 'crime enterprise', defined as 'the planned committing of offences for profit or to acquire power, which offences are each or together of major significance and are carried out by two or more persons who form a durable coop- eration with a division of labour, using commercial-like struc- tures, violence or the threat of it, or abusing political or public influence',[44] merely reflects the practical reality that organised economic crime is merely one type of entrepreneurial activity among many. Market entrepreneurs and criminal entrepreneurs are both 'market orientated'. 'They do not think in terms of national jurisdictions but in terms of flows of goods and money and in terms of the social networks of people they can trust.'[45]

Among those from whom both the entrepreneur and the crim- inal entrepreneur most seek to gain trust are the banker and the professional adviser. It is through the services provided by these practitioners that the overlap between the 'respectable' institu- tions of the upper world and the finances of the underworld become achievable, thus enabling the provenance of the 'funny' money to be disguised while corrupting the institution concerned.

The final system we wish to examine in this Part are the 'parallel' or underground banking systems. So far, the method- ologies we have discussed involve the physical movement of dirty money from its source, through a separate institutional process and onwards in an alternative, 'cleaned-up' form which it is hoped cannot be traced back to the original source money. There are other systems, however, which deserve attention, which tend to mirror more conventional clearing bank practices, and which are themselves highly efficient but wholly unauthorised methods of transferring money around the world.

Many countries, particularly in the Third World, deny their citizens the right to possess bank accounts denominated in any currency outside that of the host nation. Exchange controls are also imposed within countries where the host currency is weak in comparison with harder world currencies, in an attempt to prevent their citizens exporting their assets out of the jurisdic- tion. In most of these countries, the purchase of hard currencies such as the US dollar is normally controlled by the Central Bank, which will thus charge a premium to any person who wishes to export currency, for whatever reason. This enables the bank to make a profit on the transaction and to maintain a degree of regulatory surveillance on the activities of those who wish to transfer money abroad. In some circumstances, this need not cause any great degree of concern. Businesspeople, for example, often need to be able to have access to dollars in order to settle invoices for imports. Alternately, the 'businessperson' could just as easily be someone who is trying to export wealth from a country with an unhappy political or economic record. Neither individual wishes to pay the premium if he or she can find an alternative means of acquiring 'parallel' sources of funds, and it is in this area that the underground bankers comes into their own.

A classic example of such two-way traffic was to be seen in Colombia, before the law was changed to allow Colombian citizens the right to own and possess dollar-denominated accounts. In the past, the Colombian government imposed strict rules on the ownership of such accounts. The drug traffickers needed to be able to finance their operations at home in pesos, while having access to large sums of dollars abroad from their marketing activities. The businesspeople and those seeking capital flight services were in possession of pesos which they wanted to move to the US. The underground banker provided a natural bridge for either party. A cross transaction could be arranged, the drug trafficker depositing dollars for the businessperson in a denominated account in the United States, while a contra-entry was provided for the drug trafficker in pesos in Colombia. In neither case did any money cross a national boundary, nor was there any need for either person to run any of the inherent risks involved with the transportation of large amounts of illicit currency.

Changing the currency restriction rules, including the need for source disclosure, has meant that it has now become more profitable to exchange dollars at the banks than on the black market, a state of affairs which has produced a two-edged benefit for Colombia. While it is now one of the very few South American countries which is able to pay its foreign debt, it has now no realistic means to combat the drug traffickers' laundering activities. Colombia's economy has become literally 'drug dependent'.[46]

A similar system of parallel banking operates within Europe and the Third World under the guise of Hawala. Hawala is a

Hindi word meaning the transfer of property or information via a third party or fiduciary. Its origins pre-date conventional banking by many hundreds of years and it provides for a level of anonymity which makes supervision and control impossible. A similar system is carried on in the Far East through the 'chit' or the 'chop shop' banking facilities, both systems being conducted on similar lines.

Hawala flourishes in countries such as India which maintain stringent exchange-control regulations, and it relies upon nothing more than trust, backed up by the possession of a small piece of paper, perhaps a small denomination rupee note or even a used bus or train ticket. Any document which carries an identifiable number can be used for identification purposes. The Chinese favour small tokens such as a sugar cube with a drawing on one face. The person wishing to transfer money abroad, let us for the sake of illustration use a man in Delhi wishing to send money to his cousin in London, arranges the transaction with a Hawala broker in Delhi. He is given the numbered receipt. The broker then makes contact with another broker in London, who either deposits the relevant sum in an identifiable account there, or waits for the cousin to call on him. In the interim, the man in Delhi phones his cousin and quotes the number of the receipt, which the cousin in turn gives to the London broker. Upon receipt of confirmation that the money has been received by his cousin, the Delhi resident pays his broker, plus an agreed commission fee. The London broker records a debit entry in his books against the account of the Delhi broker, but no money is transferred between them to settle the debt. In time, the London broker will require a reverse transfer to the subcontinent and, using his contact in Delhi, the debt will be extinguished.

Hawala operates wherever there is an ethnic Indian community. NCIS maintains a watching brief on the activities of known Hawala operators because they are acutely aware of the huge sums of money such small businesses can handle, 'in many cases more cash passes through in one day than through the local bank on the corner'.[47]

The real concern for law enforcement is the increasing use of Hawala systems for laundering drug profits from the subcontinent. India is one of the world's leading staging posts on the international narcotics network, and Hawala allows many deals to be financed and transacted without any money changing hands or crossing frontiers. India smuggles gold in return for narcotics, much of the gold being illegally imported into the subcontinent by being smuggled down the Gulf from Dubai. Smuggled gold has to be paid for in hard currency and Hawala is the only means of bridging the gap between the soft and the hard currency areas. Indian government estimates show that approximately 50 billion rupees (US$3 billion) is involved in the payment for gold smuggling.[48] In return, many drug-related Hawala transactions are conducted in Dubai, like many of the Gulf States a banking area in which the handling of huge sums of cash is not considered to be at all unusual. From here, other Hawala payments can be cleared for co-partners all over the world.

Hawala relies to an extent on the generation of large sums of cash. Much of the money which was illegally syphoned out of the Johnson Matthey Bank is believed to have found its way through the Hawala system into the hands of Indian drug traffickers. Any system which enables them to generate cash is at risk, and businesses which offer commission payments will be particularly targeted. Many life and pensions companies have found themselves at risk from the activities of Hawala-related criminal enterprises who have generated large volumes of business which have been rewarded by up-front, indemnity term commission payments, only to find that much of the business was wholly fraudulent and that many of the customers were fictitious, the introducing brokerage having changed its name and disappeared.

Summary

In this necessarily brief overview of economic criminal techniques, it is worth bearing in mind that we only ever get to know a very small percentage of the criminal methods which are used in the bigger picture of economic crime. The vast majority of dishonest techniques remain hidden from view, proving that the number of variations on the methods adopted by the professionals are, as the 1985 Interim Report of the United States President's Commission on Organised Crime and Racketeering identified, 'virtually infinite and limited only by the creative imagination and expertise of the criminal entrepreneurs who devise such schemes'.

References

1. Rider, BAK (1986) 'Combating International Commercial Crime – A Commonwealth Perspective'. 4th International Symposium on Economic Crime, Jesus College, Cambridge.
2. Sutherland, E (1940) 'White Collar Criminality' *American Sociological Review*, Vol 5, No 1, Feb.
3. Rider, BAK (1990) 'Organised Economic Crime'. 8th International Symposium on Economic Crime, Jesus College, Cambridge.
4. Nye, JS (1978) 'Corruption and Political Development: A cost-benefit analysis'. In Heidenheimer, A (ed) *Political Corruption: Readings in comparative analysis.* New Brunswick.
5. Parfitt, T (1991) 'Corruption, Adjustment and African Debt'. 2nd Liverpool Conference on Fraud, Corruption and Business Crime, April.
6 Walter, I (1989) *Secret Money.* Unwin Hyman, London.
7. Rider, BAK (1992) 'Fraud in the Financial Market'. 10th International Symposium on Economic Crime, Jesus College, Cambridge.
8. Parfitt, T (1991) 'Corruption, Adjustment and African Debt'. 2nd Liverpool Conference on Fraud, Corruption and Business Crime, April.
9. Walter, I (1989) *Secret Money.* Unwin Hyman, London.
10. *The Times*, 10.8.92.
11. Sutherland, E (1949) *White Collar Crime.* Holt, Reinhart and Winston, New York.
12. Clarke, M (1990) *Business Crime: Its Nature and Control.* Polity Press, Cambridge.
13. Croall, H (1992) *White Collar Crime.* Open University Press, Buckingham.
14. Rider, BAK (1992) 'Fraud in the Financial Market'. 10th International Symposium on Economic Crime, Jesus College, Cambridge.
15. SEC (1984) *The Work of the SEC*, Washington.
16. Clarke, M (1990) *Business Crime: its Nature and Control.* Polity Press, Cambridge.
17. Rider, BAK (1979) *European Insider Dealing*, Cambridge University.
18. Walter, I (1989) *Secret Money.* Unwin Hyman, London.
19. Erdman, P (1985) *The Panic of '89.* Sphere Books, New York.

20. Box, S (1983) *Power, Crime and Mystification*. Routledge, London.
21. SEC/CFTC Publications (1982) *A Study of the Effects on the Economy of Trading in Futures and Options,* Washington, Oct 14.
22. Kaufman, H (1993) 'Financial Derivatives in a Rapidly Changing Financial World'. Talk to Skinners Hall, London.
23. Reuters, 20.1.89.
24. *Daily Telegraph*, 30.1.91.
25. Sutherland, E (1949) *White Collar Crime,* Holt, Reinhart and Winston.
26. *Money Marketing*, 10.2.94.
27. Adams, JR (1992) *A Full Service Bank*, Simon and Schuster, New York.
28. Lewis, M (1989) *Liar's Poker*, Hodder and Stoughton, London.
29. *Independent on Sunday*, 30.1.94.
30. Turk, AT (1966) 'Conflict and Criminality'. *American Sociological Review*, 31st June. 338–52.
31. Greising, D and Morse, L (1991) *Brokers, Bagmen and Moles*. Wiley, New York.
32. *Institutional Investor*, 30.1.92.
33. *Institutional Investor*, 30.1.92.
34. Kaufman, H (1993) 'Financial Deivatives in a Rapidly Changing Financial World'.
35. Poll, C Micropal Chairman. *Institutional Investor*, 30.1.92.
36. *Institutional Investor,* 30.1.92.
37. Bosworth-Davies, R and Saltmarsh, G (1994) *Money Laundering*. Chapman and Hall, London.
38. US Senate Committee on Government Affairs, 1985.
39. Rider, BAK (1993) 'Fei Ch'ien Laundries: The Pursuit of Flying Money'. *Journal of International Planning,* 1(2), 77-152.
40. United Nations (1992) 'Money Laundering and Associated Issues: The Need for International Cooperation'. UN Documents, E/CN. 15/1992/4/Add.5, 23 March, p 7.
41. *Sunday Telegraph*, 9.12.90.
42. *Financial Times*, 28.7.92.
43. DEA spokesman to the *Guardian*, 14.3.92.
44. Van Duyne, PC (1992) 'Implications of Cross-Border Crime Risks in an Open Europe'. Ministry of Justice Briefing Paper, The Hague.
45. Van Duyne, PC (1992) 'Implications of Cross-border Crime Risks in an Open Europe'. Ministry of Justice Briefing Paper, The Hague.
46. Ehrenfeld, R (1992) *Evil Money*. Harper Business, New York.
47. Interview with NCIS officer, 1993.
48. Kumar, BV (1992) 'Flight Capital Operations in the Developing World: Underground Financial Systems and Drugs and Dirty Money.' 10th International Symposium on Economic Crime, Jesus College, Cambridge.

1.2
The Role of Drugs in Organised/Economic Crime

Rowan Bosworth-Davies and Graham Saltmarsh

...in strictly economic terms, there is no relevant difference between
the provision of licit and illicit goods and services.
Robert Merton, 1957

Global mafias: The new 'corporate raiders'

Before we can begin to examine the role that narcotics now play
in underpinning the financial power base of so-called organised
crime, we believe the reader would appreciate a brief overview
of the main 'players' in this deadly game. Problem identification
and threat assessment have been a core function of the National
Criminal Intelligence Service (NCIS) since its foundation on 1
April 1992.

Indeed, 1992 can be viewed as a year when at last Europe,
with the possible exception of Italy, really woke up and took
notice of this pernicious menace. It seems now almost ironic to
the writers, in their role as observers, that for well over two
decades academics and commentators concentrated their focus
on drug abuse victims in every guise, and the distribution of drugs
into the market-place, but paid scant attention to the impact that
the burgeoning criminal economy would have upon those business and political sectors considered as untouchable, and thus
immune from the reach of the main criminal players.

During the last 20 years, trend indicators from the producer
countries gave a clue to the rest of the world community of things
to come. Those producer countries of Latin America and
Southern Asia have all experienced one or more of the following:

coup d'état, revolution, tribal tensions, violent ethnic and/or religious protest, invasion or intensive guerilla warfare. So, by default, drugs have become the principal currency for the purchase of weapons; and the human and organisational structures for the one illicit trade have come to overlap or coincide with the other. These situations were ripe for exploitation by groups of resourceful and highly intelligent criminals. However, we note that, at the time of writing, many of the same regions are experiencing an extended period of calm. This possibly confirms the theory that many governments have acquiesced to the inevitable and are now, in partnership with the cartels (always vehemently denied), reaping the benefit of the narco economy, something we should later examine and discuss.

The Research Institute for the Study of Conflict and Terrorism recently noted two important factors in the development of this phenomenon, the speed and ease of international communications and the multi-racial diversity of Western industrialised society. The migrating flows of the twentieth century have led to a wide dispersion of ethnic colonies in strategic parts of the globe, which in some cases have been activated by criminals to exploit the trust of the host country. Thus regular flights between South American and Spanish cities, human and financial transfers between the United States and Sicily, and the activities of closed Chinese communities in large Western cities – afforded cover by the overwhelming majority of their law-abiding countrymen – have provided protection for enterprise crime, currently the world's most profitable and most truly multinational activity, whose annual takings in drugs *alone* surpass world oil revenues and are second only to the arms trade.

In global terms the four main competitors are the Japanese Yakuza, the Chinese Triads, the Colombian Cartels and the Sicilian Mafia. Turkish crime groups have a virtual monopoly of the drug distribution routes from South West Asia to Europe. We will deal with Russian groups separately.

At an international level no single organisation has overall control of the illicit economy; different groups tend to dominate particular areas at different times. While ruthless competition is constant and intense, there are indications and anecdotal evidence that some unholy alliances are being struck following meetings, agreements and 'Mafia summits' between some of the main players. All realise that in a business with no recourse to written rules or courts of law, the use and maintenance of power by corruption, intimidation and violence determines the leading players, whose objectives now go way beyond the pursuit of money, and can embrace real political power in some regions. The potential for the imminent emergence of the 'criminal state' can not be understated.

This worst case scenario was succinctly put by Judge Giovanni Falcone in 1992, shortly before his assassination by the Mafia; he speculated,

> The extremely dangerous prospect of a homogenised mode of criminal organisation, in which a point is reached where one can no longer distinguish between the methods of the Yakuza, the Chinese Triads and Cosa Nostra, would create a kind of Global Mafia, and I ask myself how it could possibly be opposed. I can see this global federation taking shape.

Others also recognise this phenomena and, although caution must always be exercised when some politicians raise alarm, there can be no doubt that until 1992 the problem had been severely underplayed. Tom Wirth, the US Under-Secretary of State for Global Affairs, is quoted as saying, 'We have a problem that is accelerating far beyond the ability of our current institutions.' Senator John Kerry, Chair of the Senate Committee into Organised Crime, describes the phenomenon as 'the new communism, the new monolithic threat'.

As law enforcement officers we have watched with interest intelligence agencies and security services transferring their attention towards such criminals. Some have said that this was purely a cynical move to protect their role, if not their very existence, but the fact is that the criminal corporations pose a threat to world security, and already political control of some small nations is in the hands of organised crime.

Thus, financed with the venture capital provided by drug trafficking, social and political changes have given the cartels a new impetus to exploit the opportunities available to them for diversification. The collapse of communism starkly illustrates this issue. In the former Soviet Union and other parts of Eastern Europe, fledgling and apparently weak and indecisive governments, operating in the new free-market economy, have provided a fertile breeding ground for organised crime. This fact has not escaped the attention of the major players who, like their upper-world counterparts, want to engage in their own form of 'joint ventures'. The problem is that in this region, a blurring of distinction has occurred between the two. It is here that we are provided with our first really clear view of organised crime seeking new markets and challenges, irrespective of their legality; although whenever possible, it will seek to dominate legitimate markets by its laundered drug revenue.

As the economies of Eastern Europe develop, their lax banking laws will facilitate an entrée for the main groups who could end up owning vast tracts of the business landscape. Criminal money is frankly welcomed by some states desperate to compete in these new markets, and some governments have been offered huge loans at low interest, the sources of which at best are ambiguous. We have been involved in investigating joint ventures which have involved criminals investing at a very high level with government officials, and where the only real remedy is to wrest state assets back out of the hands of criminals by a programme of re-nationalisation, a policy of manifest political unacceptability.

The ultimate scenario as proffered by Falcone of the global mafias taking real power from democratic government could become a reality. The implications are truly terrifying, particularly now when there are clear indications that nuclear material and other lethal substances may well be falling into the hands of criminals and terrorists. By now the reader would be entitled to a severe fit of depression. There are initiatives in place and governments and agencies around the world are working together more than ever before to counter the threat, but the road will be hard and merciless.

Returning to that significant year of 1992, it was in September that the most important initiative came in identifying the problems associated with organised crime. In response to requests from Italy and France, the European Communities Ministers of Interior and Justice set up the Ad Hoc Working Group on International Organised Crime. It was constituted on a basis far wider than had been previous practice.

This pan-European working group consisted not only of police officers and officials from interested ministries, but also from the judiciary. While, as always, it had its critics, it provided for the first time a formal facility for comparing issues and for making recommendations. As a direct consequence, there can be no doubt that all European governments have finally been able to recognise all the issues and implications and have quickly come to share the view that organised crime, financed principally from the Western world's demand for narcotics, is now a significant threat to the security and stability of the region.

This has led to greater cooperation and the use of resources and the good offices of government usually reserved for other issues. In the United Kingdom the creation of a National Criminal Intelligence Service had provided a model that others now emulate and, indeed, under the Treaty of Maastricht have to create.

As has been clearly demonstrated in Italy, by marshalling the efforts of government, law enforcement and the bravery of the judiciary, with refined criminal intelligence as its engine, the ambitions and aspirations of organised crime can be capped and controlled, if not destroyed. We hope that the European views and initiatives can be emulated in states where, as we shall see, the narco dollar is achieving a status which provides short-term benefits but long-term problems.

The 'narco economy' and state dependency

There is an erroneous assumption that jurisdictions worldwide abhor trafficking in narcotics and that the policy of all governments is to eradicate the practice whenever and wherever possible. In some countries (not necessarily producer countries or merely from the Third World) there are both political and financial implications which impact upon the level of enthusiasm for applying counter-measures and the degree of commitment to contain and control trafficking worldwide.

Corruption of whole governments in producer countries is wholly viable, not to mention the concomitant corruption of the police, the military and the financial sector. Indeed, drug cultivation and processing represent a huge proportion of some states' GNP. Other countries are involved in storage and transhipment and, notwithstanding their public stance, the practical reality of their attitude to the traffickers can be described, as at best amoral pragmatism.

However, even as we write, we discern a slight change in attitude in some quarters. Politicians are coming to realise that their Faustian pacts with the traffickers could end in tears, if not more terminally, as more conventional political and less conventional criminal power plays become intertwined. This slight change of attitude is not owing to any demonstrable desire to be seen to be adopting the moral high ground, but more to do with denouncing their former friends and allies, before the very need for compliant politicians becomes in itself an irrelevance as narco power extends. It has long been said, not without some justification, that in some regions 'the monkeys are guarding the bananas'.

Of course, the nations of the Andean region personify the true extent of the narco economy and of state dependence, but this region does not necessarily have the monopoly. However, as Naylor points out, in the early to mid-1980s, Bolivia was in serious economic trouble; by 1984, per capita income had dropped 30 per cent while the inflation rate ran at 2,500 per cent. Wage increases were running at 300 per cent and the peso had depreciated from 44 to the dollar to 45,000 to the dollar. Serious trouble and a textbook case in point. [1]

Full economic collapse was prevented by coca cultivation and production fuelled by an unprecedented demand for the drug from the United States. By mid-1984, 500,000 Bolivians were dependent on the coca business. They were led by a group of former army officers who, even by South American standards, found the drugs trade significantly more rewarding than plotting coups to take over an otherwise officially bankrupt country, and who gave a new meaning to the concept of reverting to the 'cocaine standard'.

There is no doubt that the coca economy saved the country and turned it away from economic oblivion. However, the down side was that much of the cash generated did not return to Bolivia, as it was then far from possessing a safe, investable economy. And so the government and the banking system decided to go into the money laundering business (there being no relevant legislation to prevent this from happening). If the money was repatriated to Bolivia, no questions would be asked. As Naylor identified, 'the black market money of the "narcocracies" was officially invited to swallow the overground economy'. [2]

The irony is that 'officially' Bolivia is still South America's poorest nation. Yet according to the latest report by Bolivian economic analysts[3] 'international drug enforcement organisations are concerned about the high dollarisation of the [Bolivian] economy'. The report continues, '72% of current accounts, 91% of savings accounts and 91% of fixed deposits in Bolivia are in dollars'. And, perhaps not surprisingly, 'because of the high dollarisation of the [Bolivian] economy, it is very easy to introduce "coca-dollars" into the banking system'.

Not only is 'money laundering' not a crime, but banking secrecy laws prevent all law enforcement agencies from access to these accounts. The paradox for the Bolivians is that they have been saved by an illegal commodity which, in the process, kills just a few 'gringos', but that the use of its illicit profits for reinvestment is saving more traditional national activities such as tin mining (Bolivia is the world's second largest producer), copper, lead and natural gas. Recent oil discoveries, possibly bankrolled by narco dollars, have secured Bolivia's long-term recovery prospects.

Remaining in the region, Colombia of course has a long and painful record of fluctuations between state power and the influence of the drug cartels. At the time of writing, Colombian President-Elect Ernesto Samper (he took power in August 1994) has been battered by allegations of ties to the Cali Cartel, who (it is alleged) financed his presidential campaign which was fought on an anti-corruption and anti-drugs-trafficking ticket. Whatever the truth of the allegations, and they are denied by Samper, the possibility if not the probability of the Cartel's ability to reach out in this way is alarming, and has prompted US officials engaged in anti-drug operations to fear that Columbia will relax its guard against the trade in cocaine, much of which ends up in US and European cities.

As we are seeking to illustrate our points in broad terms so far as narco economy/state dependency is concerned, we now move continents to Africa. Zambia became deeply enmeshed in the drugs trade, again in the early to mid-1980s, principally as market intermediary and transit point for drugs heading to South Africa. Zambia is geographically strategic for the traffickers as it borders eight other countries. Its modern airport at Lusaka handles direct flights from Europe and India. Its police and customs are poorly paid and are potentially easily corrupted. And, as witnessed so often, as the country's economy became bankrupt through an admixture of government corruption and ineptitude, drugs became the commodity of choice for the budding entrepreneur of the narco economy.

By 1989 Kenneth Kawunda, the then president of a one-party state, gave way to international pressure and arrested and charged 25 businessmen and politicians for drugs-trafficking offences. All were subsequently acquitted. By 1991 Zambia had a democratic government but the problems did not go away; if anything they got worse. Trade in cocaine and heroin has boomed. There is a thriving market among rich white South Africans and increasingly among the newly wealthy Zambians. Money is laundered in many ways, and high-value consumer goods bought in South Africa, primarily cars, TVs and electrical goods, are stoking up a thriving black-market economy by being resold at home.

South Africa, for some obscure reason, is one of the world's biggest markets for 'Mandrax', a strong tranquilliser produced mainly in India. Such is the trade in Mandrax that it has become a *de facto* currency in Zambia; indeed, six packages each about the size of a paperback book will buy a new Toyota Corolla and for a dozen you can buy a Mercedes. There seems to be little enthusiasm to stamp out the trade, despite the passing of new laws. Indeed, allegations of corruption in the system seem to reach to the very top. Recently the former legal affairs ministers made (so far) unsubstantiated allegations that the State President, Chiluba, was receiving drugs money through an offshore trust fund.

In Asia, Thailand plans to create new drug-money laundering laws following the seizure by US officials of $10 million in assets held by a Thai politician, who they alleged headed a marijuana smuggling operation between 1977 and 1987. However, the Thai Prime Minister went on to say that 'politicians accused of drug trafficking need not necessarily show their spirit by resigning from the House [parliament] to prevent damage to the entire Parliament, as a person should be presumed innocent until proven guilty'.

In citing these examples we do not necessarily prioritise, or even criticise, a single jurisdiction any more than others; they are simply compact examples. We could have detailed case studies in Burma, China and even Hong Kong as to the extent of the narco economy. Europe itself has plenty of instances of government and financial sectors bowing to the decisions of the cartels. No one has the monopoly in duplicity. Indeed, some of the smaller dependencies of major states within the EU are in extreme danger of being overwhelmed and undermined by the narco economy. Even the UK has considered it prudent to post two highly experienced Scotland Yard officers in the Dependent Territories, the Cayman Islands, Turks & Caicos Islands, the British Virgin Islands, Anguilla and Montserrat, to prevent infiltration into the economies providing their 'off-shore financial services'.

Consequently the attention of the traffickers and law enforcement has become more focused upon Central and Eastern Europe. The attraction for the criminals is that hard Western currency is in demand on a 'no questions asked' basis. The opportunity to acquire cheaply large parts of privatisation and joint-venture schemes is an attractive prospect to organised crime with money to 'risk'. In addition the region, owing to unrest elsewhere, is finding itself part of the main transit route for heroin from Turkey and the Middle East bound for Europe. Increasingly Poland and the Czech–Slovak republics are gaining a reputation as the main producers of illegal amphetamine which, in time, could itself develop into the 'Bolivian syndrome'.

If we appear to have thus far avoided mentioning Europe in any detail, let us correct that omission now. The world's gangsters view the customer potential provided by the European market as a 'big bang' in the drugs trade, an open, borderless drugs supermarket. We are aware of an unholy alliance, if not agreement, between Colombia's Cali cartel and the Sicilian Mafia to market cocaine and launder the proceeds in Luxembourg and the Cayman Islands. About a dozen Turkish families control the European heroin trade and they cooperate with the Italian Camorra and the 'Ndrangheta in the South of Italy. Moving this stuff means official as well as criminal co-operation. The problem posed for law enforcement in Europe, despite our sophisticated police and intelligence systems with which we can often trace the actual movement of money, is that the spending intentions of the potential drug customers in Europe, upon what and in whom they may ultimately invest in the years to come, are considerably more obscure.

Narco supermarkets: regular favourites and loss leaders

> If you see a bandwagon, it's too late.
> *Sir James Goldsmith*

Organised crime discovered the single market long before politicians, financiers and industrialists. Organised crime operates in all market places, whether the commodity be drugs, human beings, toxic or nuclear material, human organs or fine art. However, it is without doubt that drugs provide the financial cornerstone of many other ventures; it generates the venture capital for a large number of other attractive propositions, not only in the underworld, but also in the upperworld economies. Consequently this key market has to be as commercial as possible and, as with any other commodity, a loyal client base has to be established.

As far as the EU is concerned, the traffickers can feel quite pleased with their market strategy; drug-related crimes account for more than half of all arrests in EU countries. There can be no doubt either that the collapse of communism and the increased exploitation of the EU single market have created vast opportunities for the criminal entrepreneurs. Traffickers and organised crime now exploit routes, both from the East and West, into the heart of Europe. Even by November 1991 it was estimated that the annual cash turnover of the Italian Mafia was more than twice that of Fiat, and about half that figure was earned by drugs. Now post-1992 we can only speculate at the numbers.

It is the level of acquisitive crime globally that gives us some idea of at least the trends of the drugs market-place. Indeed, three-quarters of all messages to and from Interpol's headquarters in Lyon concern drug-trafficking intelligence. As long ago as July 1989, France's President Mitterrand warned that 'the largest groups of drug traffickers wield power that competes directly with that of nation states'. Very useful in a free competitive environment.

Although we often hear it said that the United States' market has become saturated and that the traffickers' eyes have turned to Europe, this thesis is not all-embracing on two counts. The fact is that a saturated market of users and stocks needs to be serviced at an increasingly sophisticated level. Furthermore, particularly in the case of cocaine, Europe always has been a target, albeit initially as a 'loss leader'. Its potential was never subsequent to, or even related to the United States position, it was just another market.

The same situation is again developing in Central and Eastern Europe. The emergence of newly democratic, market-oriented governments created ready markets for the narcos, not only to set up their stalls, but to provide an increasingly steady flow of hard currency into empty central banks' coffers. As we have already indicated, this makes the latter vulnerable to trafficker corruption and/or intimidation.

While, as we believe, each market is not dependent on the other, North America is without doubt the dominant market-place, as it is in the upperworld markets. Colombia poses the biggest threat to the US and Europe. By April of 1994 European authorities had already seized over 11 metric tonnes of cocaine, compared with about 16 metric tonnes for all of 1993.

Now, not merely content with only dominating the cocaine market, Colombian drug groups are increasingly developing their capabilities to provide high-grade heroin. Intelligence shows that opium poppy cultivation in Colombia has increased dramatically. As a result, using the same personnel, routes and methods, the cartels are stepping up their efforts to ship heroin into the United States and Europe.

However, Colombian efforts thus far pale into insignificance in so far as heroin is concerned when compared to the Far East.

Burma remains the world's largest opium producer, boasting at least 70 per cent of world production. While it is recognised that most of the opium provided remains in the region for 'home market' consumption, much still finds its way to Europe and the US.

We note and indeed have experienced ourselves how easy it is to be drawn into analysis and comparisons between the US and Europe and, in so doing, to ignore other significant and growing market-places experiencing all the same problems and issues of the, by now, 'traditional' markets and routes.

Australia personifies this issue, being without doubt the prime target for cocaine, heroin and cannabis in the Pacific/Oceanic region. Much of the heroin trafficking is coordinated by Yakuza crime syndicates working in close collaboration with domestically based groups, often of ethnic Chinese descent, based in Australia. In addition, Australia continues to be a major market for South American cocaine, often flown into the country from South America via the South Pole.

There can be no doubt that Japanese crime syndicates are spreading their wings far beyond the region. There are enormous profits to be made from cocaine in Japan. To satisfy the market, the Yakuza are using Brazil as the base for their cocaine imports. Brazil houses a sizeable Japanese community which has been used by the gangsters as a shelter while they strike joint-venture partnerships with the Brazilian syndicates. Reports from Interpol indicate that Japan remains the principal market for methamphetamine manufactured in China, Taiwan and South Korea, all of this orchestrated by the Yakuza, who clearly have global drug-trafficking ambitions.

However, just like all markets there is a discernable, albeit small, change in consumption patterns, together with an increase in seizures worldwide. Again it is market behaviour that begins to give us trend indications. We note much of the rhetoric about 'losing the war against drugs' and we accept neither the hypothesis nor the philosophy. There has never been a 'war' against drugs. We, in the main, have combated this market with criminal justice measures within a democratic framework, together with education programmes. Just as there are signs of the market changing, some ill-informed yet senior individuals seek to legalise, or at least rationalise, some of the issues. We say, as ever, 'look at the market- place'. The fact is the use of cocaine in the United States and Europe has probably peaked and may be in decline. Newsweek[4] quoted an experienced anti-drug specialist at Interpol as saying, 'It's a terrible thought, but we may just put ourselves out of business by the end of the decade'. While we do not necessarily subscribe to that extent, we do note that the cartels are changing tack. Drug consumption in Eastern and Central Europe is increasing, no doubt influenced by the traditional cartels in cooperation with other more local crime groups, an issue we shall discuss shortly. Perhaps the most compelling evidence of this was the recent seizure in St Petersburg of a ton of cocaine from Colombia *en route* from Finland. According to Russian law enforcement, it was the product of Colombian, Israeli and Russian criminal collaboration.

Eastern Europe, particularly the former Soviet Union, provides a pot-pourri of organised crime/drug-trafficking activity. Paradoxically it was their facilities for money laundering that set the pace, as lax banking laws initially attracted organised crime, not just because they offered a safe haven for the money, but because they could also be used as a venture capital base for investing in the newly privatised infrastructure of these newly 'democratic' states. This was quickly followed by the recognition of the potential of Eastern Europe as a perfect transhipment route into Western Europe. Finally, it offered a huge potential end-user market for drugs in the same way as any other 'Western' consumer product, such as McDonald's, Coca Cola and Marlboro cigarettes, could be profitably marketed. The paradox here was that the phenomenon came about in reverse order.

Even if this were not bad enough, apart from routing and general drug trafficking, the potential drug-crop production of the Kazakhstan–Tajikistan area cannot but be of concern. This remote region, containing as it does great tracts of its own drug-producing areas, has the potential, for the first time, to create a wholly self-sufficient drug production, trafficking and money laundering loop, with little immediate prospect of law enforcement intervention.

And so the drugs market, like any other, adapts and mutates

and the concerns of today evaporate as we recognise the problems of tomorrow.

> The dogs bark, but the caravan passes on.
> *Mohamed Fayed 14.3.90*

Underworld mergers and acquisitions

> It is a natural part of the evolution of
> corporate entities that the strong should eat
> the weak; to the strong should go the rewards.
> *Roger Seelig*

The concern over the 'globalisation' of organised crime is well founded. While, at least at present, there is no single worldwide criminal conspiracy in such a vast market-place, it is only natural that interested parties should at least collaborate with each other. This is no more different than an upperworld analogy of the Ford Motor Company and Nissan making the same four-wheel-drive vehicle, but targeting a separate market, or even, on occasions, the same market where demand exceeds supply.

Although in its embryonic stage, there is no doubt that international criminal cooperation is occurring. All of this in time will lead to mergers and takeovers, although they promise to be more dramatic than the average boardroom coup. In her book *Crime Without Frontiers*, Claire Sterling notes that the collapse of the Soviet Empire has brought the big crime groups of East and West together and that the Sicilian and American Mafias in particular are now 'working with their counterparts in Eastern Europe and the former Soviet Union'.[5] The US State Department's Irving Soloway is quoted in 1993 as confirming that the leaders of these groups have met in Warsaw in 1991, in Prague in 1992 and in Berlin in 1993. There 'they agreed to apply strategic planning and market development policies for the new emerging free markets, to programme legitimate investments much as corporations do and to develop and expand extremely illegal activities besides'.

There is no doubt that both the reality and the concepts of organised crime, nationally and globally, were transformed by the catalyst of the collapse of the former Soviet Union. While it is certainly not helpful to sensationalise the risks, the subsequent criminal events became a high agenda item, not only for international law enforcement, but for the competing cartels themselves.

Eastern and Central European groups sell weapons to the Sicilian Mafia. In 1993 a further conference was held in Paris between Italian and Japanese crime bosses to discuss areas of 'mutual interest'. As these groups merge and carve up the markets, more local groups of criminals are likely to be annihilated in much the same way as a supermarket destroys the trade of a corner grocery store, except that the process is likely to be more violent.

As we have already indicated, the core commodity is, and will remain, narcotics, and the vast sums generated globally will enter the global financial system and institutional investment portfolios. Estimates vary, but the Organization for Economic Co-operation and Development says that at least $85 billion in drug profits go into the financial markets each year.

For some years there was anecdotal evidence that both the American and Italian 'Mafias' had been eased out of the narcotics trade by the Colombian Cartels and some Turkish groups. In fact, nothing could be further from the truth. Although the Mafias may not have ultimate control of the drugs market globally, their home bases are strong and, in collaboration with groups from producer countries, are still significant distributors worldwide. Utilising the flexibility and complexity that any major corporation has to adopt, the traditional mafias have diverged into both the upperworld and underworld economies in a variety of ways. Today the Mafia need not buy bankers and accountants – it owns some very big banks and corporations, not just in Italy and America.

As Sterling reports,[6] the Camorra and Mafia have been installed along the French Riviera for decades. A special commission of the French parliament reported in 1993 reported the existence of an organisational grouping of some 30 companies in Europe, the US, South America, Panama and the island of Saint Martin, with perfect logistics for transport over a good part of the planet.

In February 1993, Russian President Boris Yeltsin confessed,

'Nearly two-thirds of Russian commercial structure had ties to the growing criminal world.' At this juncture we should point out that, although we see the realisation of organised crime from Eastern Europe as a catalyst for governmental panic world-wide, organised crime in Russia or the Soviet satellites is hardly a new phenomenon in the region's history. Indeed, even in the early days there was a spirit of cooperation and coexistence. In the communist era, criminal groups' use of extortion and black-market activity functioned almost as an extension of the Communist Party and the KGB, who used a 'second economy' for their own purposes. Brezhnev was content to allow an alter-native 'black-market' economy to thrive on an unofficial 'blind-eye' basis, because it was one of the few ways the official, centralised Russian economy had of providing a rudimentary system of exchange, albeit one to which only the most politi-cally or criminally privileged had access. Now these same groups have mutated, merely outliving the state that spawned them.

The oxygen to any organised crime grouping is the ability to infiltrate government, the judicial and financial systems. Consequently, upon the fall of communism the Russian groups had a market advantage, as they still had their allies in the state infrastructure. This is where their power lies and why they are so frightening in the home base. Links were forged between Russian and Italian groups to move money through the Russian banking system, and now these same groups own not just compa-nies, but whole corporations and banks throughout Eastern Europe and Russia.

A result of the 1992 Mafia 'summit' was an agreement that the Italians would provide the 'know-how' to acquire and distribute drugs, while the Russians would provide security for transit routes and the distribution networks. However, such a continuing partnership between the Italian and Russian Mafias will undoubtedly increase the international trafficking in weapons, toxic materials and possibly nuclear material and components, although thus far the latter category, in the main, has been little more than scams.

The world's appetite for drugs will continue to distort the global economy for the foreseeable future, despite some chinks of light here and there. The amounts of money generated from just this one form of criminal activity are unprecedented in the history of civilisation. While there are struggles to dominate the market-place, the kingpins, for the moment at least, have found collaboration rather than confrontation more profitable. However this uneasy coexistence is unlikely to last for too long, political power and market dominance will transcend the business treaties in due course. All of the main players have demonstrated their ability to reach out and destroy anything or anyone who gets in their way. Where the legal or financial system thwarts their aims, they will create their own alternatives with resources which are the envy of many governments in the free world.

The most worrying factor in global criminal cooperation is the dangerous coexistence of the cartels with politics and the impact they can make upon the markets. Yet when the politicians of some states can no longer be bought, or are removed, the criminal organisations react to state attacks with bombs and guns. The Mafia are prepared to argue through the use of terrorism, to take on state systems and, in some jurisdictions, take them over. Consequently the struggle against organised crime requires a clear perception of the organisation, coupled with sound intelligence and a resolve to break their power.

The international response: preventing a hostile take-over

> We are soldiers in a global war.
> *Peter Morgan*

The richer and developed countries are far better equipped to deal with the effects of transnational organised crime than those poorer countries who, of course, suffer far more from its impact. It is the legitimate system and a strong economy that ultimately cap and control organised crime, although at the same time they provide paradoxically a happy hunting-ground for economic crime, fraud and money laundering.

Certainly the governments of Western Europe, the United States, Canada and Australia are demonstrating that they are far from powerless in dealing with organised and economic crime, but we do not share the despondency regarding the perceived futility in tackling drug trafficking. Nobody ever said it was going to be easy. We are beginning to fight back, which is why we noted and consider the European Ad Hoc Working Group to be so significant. We consider it to be a model for law enforcement, jurists and academic aims. It was formed following a meeting on 18 September 1992 of Interior and Justice Ministers of the EU member states in Brussels, to discuss the possibility of enhancing joint action to 'address the serious and growing problem of international organised crime'.

The ministers decided to set up an Ad Hoc Working Group of police and judicial experts, with a mandate to report within six months on the organisations and structures of the Mafia and other international criminal organisations, then with a view to incorporating its recommendations into the cooperation structures to be set up after the coming into force of the Maastricht Treaty. The Ad Hoc Group held a series of meetings in London and Copenhagen, with a final drafting meeting in Rome. The Organised Crime Unit of the UK National Criminal Intelligence Service formed part of the UK delegation.

The Working Group was tasked with the following aims:

- to identify the nature and structure of the Mafia and other international criminal organisations and the extent of their activity within member states;
- to assess the threat which organised crime poses to member states from both within and outside the EU;
- to assess what action has already been taken against international organised crime and comment on its relevance;
- to comment on the effectiveness of co-ordination between ongoing activities and note any gaps in provision and to make recommendations to ministers.

The final report contained a wide range of recommendations to ministers in such areas of closer cooperation and exchange of information. Extradition and customs cooperation initiatives were also recommended and are being considered.

The European Union as such has no authority in the area of criminal law. Thus the role of combating international organised crime remains solely within the competence of the member states.

Prior to the creation of the Ad Hoc Working Group and following a German proposal at the Luxembourg European Council in June 1991, 'Europol' was accorded recognition and is now a working reality based in The Hague. However, it is a different animal to that imagined by Chancellor Helmut Kohl. A ministerial agreement establishing Europol initially as a drugs unit (EDU) was signed in Copenhagen in June 1993. Its foundation envisages a system (within the EU region) of information exchange to prevent and combat terrorism, drug traffickers and other serious crime in the region. Interpol remains unaffected in its global role of information and intelligence exchange, together with its coordination role for international operations. Neither, of course, is operational nor has any power to *direct* investigators.

Consequently the Mafia and other groups can plan the crime in one jurisdiction, commit it in another, flee to yet one more and then launder the proceeds anywhere in the world, and watch as investigators become submerged in judicial bureaucracy and disputes. It is to be hoped that much of this will at least be addressed by the developed nations as global, political and economic changes continue to present opportunities to the bad guys.

It is a matter of coordination, not simply between jurisdictions, but by competing international agencies; not just police and customs, but by the security services across the region who certainly have their part to play. This is where, given the political will and finance, organisations such as the UK's National Criminal Intelligence Service have such an important role as the 'honest broker'.

Moving further afield, the United States Senate Sub-Committee on Terrorism, Narcotics and International Operations sitting in April 1994 accrued valuable evidence from those called before it. They have been told that the strategy to combat the phenomenon must be inter-agency, multidisciplinary and *international*. This global strategy has to address urgently the critical issues, including jurisdictional questions among agencies and the collection and sharing of information between the intelligence community, law enforcement and financial regulators.

There is now no doubt that there *is* an international commitment to the strategy. Regional variations are being recognised and accommodated and there is more flexibility between investigating jurisdictions, although, as always, more can be achieved. Various studies are identifying the different ways that money can be laundered globally. There is a greater awareness of the difficulties some states have in covert operations, telephone intercepts, the recruiting and use of informants, etc.

Giving evidence to the Senate hearing, the Director of the CIA pointed out the main difference between the challenge posed by international crime and that posed by nations who had previously been adversaries. He said:

> As a rule, nations do not exist in a constant state of conflict. Even during the long struggle of the cold war, when co-operation was not feasible, communication was possible. From quiet diplomacy to public *démarches*, from hot lines to summiting, the means could be found to try to settle disputes. Often the negotiating table was just a phone call away.
>
> With organised crime there is no such table. The tools of diplomacy have no meaning to groups whose business revolves around drug trafficking, extortion and murder. And when international organised crime can threaten the stability of regions and the very viability of nations, the issues are far from being exclusively in the realm of law enforcement; they also become a matter of national security.[7]

Conclusion

Quite clearly the prognosis is for more, rather than less transnational collaboration among criminal groups. As the global economy integrates, both legal and illegal businesses will exploit every opportunity. The sheer scale and dynamics of transnational, if not global, crime will force the main players into unholy alliances and partnerships as we have described, citing the Colombian/Italian example as perhaps the most worrying, transhipping cocaine to Europe under an 'umbrella' agreement in such matters as delivery, price and distribution policy.

Increased international law enforcement activity is having very positive results and the doomsday scenario is firmly rejected. Organised crime can never be eradicated, but it can be capped and controlled. However, there is much left to be done, not least in assisting our less well-off neighbouring states with expertise, guidance and sometimes 'encouragement'. For the work against the mafias is resource intensive and expensive, requiring talented and skilled personnel to be able to travel and operate with the same freedom as their quarry.

On a diplomatic front, countries such as the Bahamas, Colombia and Russia must be persuaded to pass anti-money-laundering laws. Other territories and money havens who prostitute themselves in order to handle criminal monies must be sanctioned and shamed.

No one body of expertise or jurisdiction will defeat the cartels' dedicated criminal intelligence; close international cooperation and trust just might, but the road will be long and painful as our very brave colleagues in Italy have shown us. We owe it to them to prove that their sacrifices have not been in vain.

References

1. Naylor, RT (1987) *Hot Money and the Politics of Debt*. Unwin Hyman, London.
2. Naylor, RT (1987) *Hot Money and the Politics of Debt*. Unwin Hyman, London.
3. Muller and Associates (1994) 'Behaviour and Assessment of the Banking System'. May.
4. *Newsweek*, 13.12.93.
5. Sterling, C (1994) *Crime Without Frontiers*. Little, Brown, London.
6. Sterling, C (1994) *Crime Without Frontiers*. Little, Brown, London.
7. Woolsey, RJ, Director CIA, 20.4.94.

1.3
The Application of IT and Electronic Communications to Facilitate Fraud*

Rowan Bosworth-Davies and Graham Saltmarsh

*We gratefully acknowledge the contribution to the this chapter made by Gurpreet Dillon and Dr James Buckhouse of the Computer Security Reasearch Centre, Information Systems Department, London School Of Economics & Political Science

> For knowledge itself is power.
> *Sir Francis Bacon, 1561–1626*

The international revolution in financial services, resulting in the creation of the 24-hour market in which investment instruments can be traded around the world, across the time zones, on an electronic network which never sleeps, was inspired and facilitated primarily by the development of information and communications technology. The vital ingredient for successful, profitable trading in financial products is information: information on company results, whether bad or good; interest rates, are they rising or falling; commodity prices; stock and bond values; currency fluctuations. All market traders rely on being able to access the latest accurate information on these and a myriad of other factors which impact upon the immediacy of the decision whether they should buy or sell, and the most important element of their access to this information is the speed with which it can be obtained. The development of the computer and the rest of the accompanying high-tech, cyber-space electronic wizardry has not only given the market trader the speed and the access he or she requires, but has gone much further, by providing the means to design the new 'derivatives' products which are now providing a new dimension in financial risk management and taking the money manipulators into realms of technical possibility hitherto undreamed of.

However, the *alter ego* of the legitimate user of this technological revolution, the fraudster, has also kept pace with the speed of change. In the same way that the computer can be used to create profit for its lawful user, it can be used just as effectively to commit crime by its criminal owner. The professional fraudster is incapable of seeing a new piece of IT equipment without wondering how it could be used to facilitate a new kind of fraud.

At the same time, nevertheless, there is a great danger that the risks from the hacker or the techno-bandit can be overstated, leading to a level of fear of 'computer crime' which is simply not justified by the evidence to support its existence. More computer-related losses are caused to business through employee incompetence, technical failure or hardware corruption by external sources, than are created by the computer criminal. It is important, therefore, to be able to put the IT revolution into context when considering its contribution to the economic crime debate and, at the same time, to consider how important computer security has become as a means of denying access to the criminal or the network abuser.

IT systems are highly cost-intensive products to research, develop, market and maintain. The costs involved in underwriting the primary development of the technical financial support systems have been borne, to a large extent, by the major banks who pioneered the use of computerised accounting systems to facilitate their financial clearing systems. When individual financial transactions in the major world currencies running into many millions of dollars have become a daily norm among the developed free-market economies, one of the most important cost-related factors for end-users of these transaction systems is the delay which they experience during the 'clearing' of the transaction. The ideal situation for the international banking system would be the creation of a 'real-time', same-day system of settlement, in which monies being transferred could be systematically debited from the referring account and credited to the receiving account, in their respective currencies, as soon as the transaction occurred, thus avoiding the creation of intra-day debit positions.

Ten years ago, the concept of a same-day, sterling settlement system and the associated risks from a failure within automated bank payments networks were causing considerable concern to the Bank for International Settlements:

> The major change in the last ten years has been the replacement of account-based systems by customer-based information systems. These in turn have provided a basis for a wide range of database marketing activities. Real-time processing has become the norm for many transactions (in fund management as well as banking).[1]

The competition between the rather narrow range of software producers to design user packages for back-office administration systems has led to fierce product marketing campaigns, generating increased research and development investment.

> The bank-owned SWIFT network has been transformed during the last ten years. In 1983, SWIFT was a utility for banks to exchange one-off payments instructions. Today, it provides messages for the securities industry; plays a role in global custody; offers a vehicle for EDI (Electronic Data Interchange) messaging and will carry bulk files for banks wishing to make mass payments across international frontiers.[2]

But as computer-facilitated communications systems have helped to revolutionise the financial netmap, at the same time as assisting in the commission of fraud, they have been used to create a new dimension in criminal behaviour, although the distinction between crimes committed by computers as opposed to crimes committed with the help of computers is still blurred. Computer crime is described as 'low risk – high reward', but the damage which can be caused to the commercial viability of a business which is infiltrated by a computer criminal is very high indeed.

Computer crime can cover a very wide field of egregious activity. It can be used to commit fraud, as where a dishonest person leaves computerised instructions for the payment of sums of money to an unauthorised account. The most well-known, and possibly apocryphal, example of this 'salami slicing' was the case involving the junior employee of a bank who instructed the bank's accounting computer to round each customer's account down to the nearest 5 cents, transferring the maximum of 4 cents thus created in each calculation to his own account. It can be used to commit theft: theft of information from a company's records can be extremely valuable in the hands of an industrial spy or someone planning a corporate takeover. It can be used to steal money from an account, as where an unauthorised person uses another's personal code number to access the latter's bank account and withdraw cash. A significant cause of concern to banks and financial institutions is the possibility of the infiltration of their staff members by a criminal from an organised crime or terrorist group, whose access to its computerised facilities places the company at considerable risk. An example was uncovered in London in 1993, where a female computer systems analyst employed by a major financial institution was convicted of attempting to obtain £1.6 million. She was willing to work late at night and at weekends in an unsupervised capacity, although no one within the company bothered to check that all the work she claimed to have carried out was genuine. Subsequent enquiries revealed that she had a wide network of criminal associates, many of whom were living in Spain, and she had been part of a criminal gang which was engaged in transferring credits from discretionarily managed client accounts to criminally owned accounts abroad.

Another example of computer-related fraud was where a fraudster found a way to bypass the security systems on what had hitherto been thought of as an impenetrable electronic funds transfer system which handles up to £100 billion a day. The Clearing House Automated Payments System (CHAPS), which used standardised banking computer software, was financed by a consortium of major banks, all of which made use of its services. It was infiltrated by a man using a false name, which was made possible by the absence of any mandatory checks on the identity of those who collected cash payments made as a result of a CHAPS transfer. Prior to the theft taking place, the fraudster opened a bank account with a small branch bank which was intended to receive the cash payments. He then cleverly forged the signatures of the directors of a company in another part of the country which banked with its own local branch of a bank from another banking chain. The letter instructed the company's bank to transfer £39,000 to the fraudster's waiting account at a specified date and time. The CHAPS transfer avoided the necessity for the transferred cheque to be cleared and the man was able to walk into the bank and take the sum out in cash within half an hour of it arriving in the account.

The most commonly used word to describe unauthorised use of computer systems is 'hacking'. The activity covers a wide variety of egregious behaviour which can range from unauthorised access to telecommunications networks (the obtaining of free telephone calls); through unauthorised access to other computer systems (such as a university's computerised library systems or the records of public utilities); through the dishonest use of credit card numbers for making unauthorised purchases of goods; ending up with the leaving of destructive computer 'viruses' within another user's computer system, otherwise referred to as 'computer terrorism'.

More recently, another word has crept into the computer lexicon, 'cracking', which describes the hacking activities of persons or institutions whose actions are deliberately intended to be for a dishonest motive. One of the most headlined examples was where Virgin Airlines claimed that British Airways' staff had dishonestly hacked into the Virgin computer system to access data on Virgin's customer base, and then had used that information to target those clients with attractive offers to encourage them to transfer their custom to British Airways.

In America, the Federal Bureau of Investigation is looking into widespread allegations of 'cracking' on the Internet system, which carries highly confidential information between banks, embassies, government departments and universities from around the world. Many credit card transactions are frequently routed on the system for verification by banks and retailers. The crackers have gained access to user passwords, and have been able to unlock credit card details by using highly sophisticated programs called 'sniffers'.

Computerised communications systems facilitate fraud in exactly the same way as they facilitate the honest use for which they have been devised, for the simple reason that all fraud, whether committed by a fountain pen or by a computer, is indistinguishable from ordinary, legal behaviour, and is based upon nothing more than a deceitful breach of trust. The addition of the computer into the fraud equation introduces an additional psychological barrier for the user, because once the initial technical problems associated with process unfamiliarity are overcome, we quickly develop a tendency to accept what the computer tells us. This 'willing suspension of disbelief' encourages us to accept instructions or processes which occur within the computerised system without question, particularly when those instructions or answers do not give the appearance of being outside the expected norm.

A good illustration of this phenomenon occurred in Britain in the immediate aftermath of the introduction of the police national computer facility to record lost or stolen motor vehicles. A policeman could call his station and obtain an immediate computer check on the status of a suspect vehicle. Ironically, the introduction of this facility led to a reduction in the number of lost or stolen vehicles being recovered. The 'street intuition' of the police officer, which had led to suspicion of the car or its driver in the first place, was assuaged if he or she was told that the computer contained no report concerning the vehicle. Prior to the introduction of the computer, the police officer would have questioned the driver closely and in many cases might have discovered that the car had only been recently stolen, but the report of a negative computer search often resulted in no questioning being undertaken.

Thus if perceived information validity is one of the potential weak links in the chain of computer-user risk, then one of the most important elements for combating computer-related fraud is the considered implementation of effective computer security systems, which enable the system user to be able to guarantee a far greater likelihood of the integrity of the information being accessed. It is to a more detailed examination of this topic that we now wish to turn. We are very grateful to our friends Gurpreet Dillon and Dr Jim Backhouse from the Computer Security Centre of the London School of Economics for their contribution to this part of the chapter.

Computer fraud: its management and control

In the last two years, computer fraud has taken its toll on businesses in the UK to the tune of £1.2 billion because of inadequate security.[3] This is in contrast to the 1993 company expenditure on information technology which exceeded £12 billion.[4] A survey by the UK Local Government Audit Commission revealed that 41 per cent of the reported incidents were fraud (others being theft, hacking and virus attacks). Astonishingly, 60 per cent of the frauds were detected by accidental means. The average cost for a security breach has been estimated at £9,361, although the most costly single incident was a £1.2million fraud in an insurance company.[5] Indeed, the widespread use of information technology (IT) by businesses today has given rise to new forms of illicit behaviour and 'security blindness' on the part of the users.[6]

Against this background of computer-related fraud, businesses and organisations are still trying to cope with the intricacy and mystique that surrounds computer systems. It appears that far less security is applied to data held in computer systems than is the case for data held in manual systems. Office workers are familiar with the security requirements of a filing cabinet, but not necessarily those of a computer system. In the corporate world, computer security is generally seen as being of interest to the IT department, and so many professionals do not give adequate importance to these security concerns of an organisation. Even if they do, they come up with solutions that are overcomplicated. Our main premise is that more proactive security administration is needed: it argues that many of the losses owing to fraud could be avoided if businesses were more serious about prevention and deterrence.

The phenomenon of computer fraud

The Audit Commission has defined computer fraud as 'any fraudulent behaviour connected with computerisation by which someone intends to gain dishonest advantage'. The breadth of this definition not only permits us to consider a wide range of cases where different means have been used to carry out a fraud-ulent activity, but also to regard computer frauds as 'frauds first and foremost, and the use or abuse of a computer . . . as a secondary matter'.[7]

Computer fraud falls into three broad categories: input, throughput and output fraud. Input frauds are the easiest to commit and are carried out by entering false or manipulated information into the computer systems. There are numerous examples of this kind of fraud. Recently the Audit Commission reported a case where £68,000 was deliberately diverted into an inappropriate bank account. The perpetrator, who was an employee of the central government department, set up a fake 'supplier file' on the costing system, retained the correct name and address, but changed the bank details to those of a private individual. The internal controls failed to spot the new supplier file details, and consequently it was authorised without checking. This is a typical example of an input fraud carried out by 'posi-tive falsification' and involves the actual insertion of additional data.[8] There are also instances of 'negative falsification' where the input data is suppressed, so that the computer does not process it.

Throughput frauds are, however, the most difficult to execute. One needs good technical expertise and a significantly high level of access. The most commonly cited example is the 'salami slicer' who manipulates a large number of accounts to slice off small amounts (although there are few reported sightings of this exotic mythical beast). One interesting case came to light when a bank clerk, in charge of foreign exchange currency desk, fed false exchange rates into the purchases/creditors system. Each day this resulted in a false excess cash position which was pocketed by the clerk.[9] Internal control mechanisms attributed the blame to poor system development and other related procedures.

Frauds such as this can easily be prevented by simple tech-nical and formal controls. At a technical level, a good piece of software capable of carrying out self-validation can act as a deterrent. Formal structures in the form of explicit reporting arrangements and organisational rules would provide further support. For instance, most financial transactions are governed by explicit rules, thus making it relatively easy to forecast various parameters. Consequently it is also easy to identify any exceptional behaviour. If an organisation has a formal reporting structure in place, the responsible person can be forewarned. In France, such controls have played an important role in bringing about a dramatic decrease in credit card fraud, from $121 million in 1991 to $52 million in 1993. The success is attributed to rigid technical controls, implemented by the use of 'smart card' technology, and formal organisational and administrative structures to support these technical measures.

The third category of frauds is the falsification of outputs. This occurs to conceal bogus input and to postpone detection. These frauds are relatively unsophisticated and are not as common as other kinds of falsification.[11] This is largely because there are very few opportunities available, since most vulnerabilities have been identified and controls established. However, even though the controls seem to work, there is still room for improvement. For example, in one financial institution, a branch cashier was motivated to falsify members' investment accounts.[12] She stole money from the till, entered false withdrawals into the accounts and destroyed the audit rolls from the printers along with the withdrawal forms. She was, however, unaware that an audit trail of branch transactions was regularly recorded at the principal office. Investigations revealed that the opportunity to defraud existed because formal transaction-control mechanisms were not harmonised. The transactions were not numbered, numeric sequences were not checked and missing transactions were not investigated.

What is emerging is the belief that, to contain incidents of computer fraud, the organisation must implement adequate controls. Whatever the nature of computer frauds (input, throughput or output), technical and formal controls are not enough, especially when growth in information and communication technologies has detached employees from their principal places of work. The concepts of teleworking and contracting out are fast taking root; there is a growing trend in Western economies to outsource most organisational functions from garbage collection to IT services. The following section identifies the range of possible controls that could be established to prevent computer fraud.

Controlling computer fraud

Control is 'the use of interventions by a controller to promote a preferred behaviour of a system-being-controlled'.[13] Thus organisations which seek to contain computer fraud would strive to implement a broad range of interventions. These can be classified into three categories: technical, formal and informal. Typically an organisation can implement controls to limit access to buildings, rooms or computer systems (technical controls). Commensurate with this, the organisational hierarchy could be expanded or shortened (formal controls) and an education, training and awareness programme put in place (informal or pragmatic controls).

In practice, however, controls have dysfunctional effects. The most important reason is that isolated solutions (ie controls) have been provided for specific problems. These 'solutions' tend to ignore other existing controls and their contexts. Thus individual controls in each of the three categories, though important, must complement each other. This necessitates an overarching policy which determines the nature of controls being implemented and therefore provides comprehensive security to the organisation.

Essentially, the focus of any security policy is to create a shared vision and an understanding of how various controls will be used, so that data and information in an organisation are protected. The vision is shared among all levels in the organisation and uses people and resources to impose an environment that is conducive to the success of an enterprise. Typically an organisation would develop a security policy based on a sound business judgement, the value of data being protected and the risks associated with the protected data. It would then be applied in conjunction with other enterprise policies: corporate policy on disclosure of information and personnel policy on education and training.

In choosing the various requirements of a security policy, it is extremely difficult to draw generalisations. Since the security policy of an enterprise largely depends upon the prevalent organisational culture, the choice of individual elements is case specific. However, as a general rule of thumb all security policies will strive to implement controls in the three areas discussed above. Let us now examine each in more detail.

Technical controls

Today businesses are eager to grasp the idea of implementing complex technological controls to protect the information held in their computer systems. Most of these controls have been in the area of access control and authentication. A particularly exciting development has been smart card technology which is being extensively used by the financial sector.[14] However, authentication methods have made a great deal of progress. It has now been recognised that simple password protection is not enough, and so there is the need to identify the individual (i.e. is the user the person he/she claims to be?). This has to some extent been accomplished by using the sophisticated 'challenge-response box' technology. The challenge-response box contains an encryption algorithm with the facility for setting up a key. The computer then sends a random number to the user, who is required to encrypt it and send it back to the system. The response is then compared with the 'locally encrypted' version. Access is granted when there is a complete match.

There have been other developments such as block ciphers,[15] which have been used to protect sensitive data. There has been particular interest in message authentication, with practical applicability in the financial services and banking industry. Furthermore, the use of techniques such as voice analysis and digital signatures has strengthened technology-oriented security controls. Ultimately implementation of technological solutions is dependent upon cost justifying the controls.

Although technological controls are essential in developing safeguards around sensitive information, the effectiveness of such technological solutions is questionable. The perpetrators 'generally stick to the easiest, safest, simplest means to accomplish their objectives, and those means seldom include exotic, sophisticated methods.'[16] For instance, it is far easier for a criminal to obtain information by overhearing what people say or finding what has been written on paper, than by electronic eavesdropping. In fact, in the last four decades there has hardly been any proven case of eavesdropping on radio frequency emanations.[17] Therefore, before implementing technological controls, business enterprises should consider constituting well-developed, baseline organisational controls (eg vetting, allocating responsibilities, awareness).

Formal controls

Technological controls require adequate organisational support. Consequently rule-based formal structures need to be put in place. These determine the consequences of misinterpretation of data and misapplication of rules in an organisation, and help in allocating specific responsibilities. At an organisational level, development of a 'task-force' helps in carrying out security management and give a strategic direction to various initiatives. Ideally the task-force should have representatives from a wide range of departments such as audit, personnel, legal and insurance. Ongoing support should be provided by computer security professionals. Besides these, significant importance should be given to personnel issues. Failing to consider these adequately could result in disastrous consequences. It has been reported[18] that most computer fraud is carried out by employees of the organisation (an astonishing 61 per cent). The actual figure is certainly higher, since only 9 per cent of cases have been positively linked with outsiders.

Thus formal controls should not only address hiring procedures but also the structures of responsibility during employment. A clearer understanding of the structures of responsibility helps in the attribution of blame, responsibility, accountability and authority. It goes without saying that the honest behaviour of the employees is influenced by their motivation. Therefore it is important to inculcate a subculture which promotes fair practices and moral leadership. The greatest care, however, should be taken over the termination practices for employees. It is a well-documented fact that most cases of computer fraud occur shortly before the employee leaves the organisation.

Finally, the key principle in assessing how many resources to allocate to security (technical or formal controls) is that the amount spent should be in proportion to the criticality of the system, cost of remedy, and the likelihood of the breach of security occurring. It is necessary for the management of organisations to adopt appropriate controls to protect themselves from claims of negligent duty and also to comply with the requirements of data-protection legislation.

Pragmatic controls

Increasing awareness of security issues is the most cost-effective control for an organisation. It is often the case that IT security is presented to the users in a form that is beyond their comprehension, and it is thus a demotivating factor in implementing adequate controls.[19] Increased awareness should be supplemented by an ongoing education and training programme. Such training and awareness programmes are extremely important in developing a 'trusted' core of members of the organisation. The emphasis should be to build an organisational subculture where it is possible to understand the intentions of the management. An environment should also be created which is conducive to developing a common belief system. This would make members of the organisation committed to their activities. All this is made possible by adopting good management practices. Such practices have special relevance in organisations today, since they are moving towards outsourcing key services and thus have an increased reliance upon third parties for infrastructural support.[20] This has consequences of increased dependency and vulnerability for the organisation, thereby increasing the probability of risks.

The first step in developing good management practices and reducing the risk of fraud is adopting some baseline standards, the importance of which has been highlighted earlier. In the UK, the Department of Trade and Industry has taken the initiative to develop such a code. It intends to provide a common basis for developing and implementing effective security management practices so that there is an increased confidence in inter-organisational transactions.

Conclusion

It goes without saying that the prevention of computer fraud is more effective than its treatment. Implementing controls, as identified in a security policy, would indeed deter computer misuses. At an organisational level this can be achieved by identifying the 'rotten apples in the barrel'. In spite of this, fraud by insiders remains a problem, and at times high-tech insider fraud can be difficult to prevent, especially if it blends with legitimate transactions. It can, however, be prevented to some extent by having good baseline controls. Appropriate legislative controls and stricter criminal penalties would also act as deterrents.

Adequate reporting of incidents of fraud might help us to build a clearer picture of the problem. This would be beneficial in the long term. Ultimately if organisations develop a security policy which gives equal consideration to technical, formal and pragmatic controls, it would be possible to minimise losses from computer fraud.

References

1. *Financial Technology International Bulletin*, September 1993.
2. *Financial Technology International Bulletin*, September 1993.
3. Yazel, L (1994) 'The high price of insecurity'. *Computing*, 21 April, p23.
4. Willcocks, L and Lester, S (1993) 'Evaluation and control of IS investments: recent UK survey evidence'. Research and discussion paper No. RDP93/3, Oxford Institute of Information Management, Templeton College, Oxford.
5. Yazel, L (1994) 'The high price of insecurity'. *Computing*, 21 April, p23.
6. Hurford, C (1989) 'Computer Fraud – The UK Experience'. *The Computer Bulletin*, pp19–20.
7. Simons, G (1989) *Viruses, Bugs and Star Wars*. NCC Blackwell, Manchester.
8. West, H (1987) *Fraud: the growth industry*. British Institute of Management, London.
9. Audit Commission (1990) *Survey of Computer Fraud and Abuse.*' The Audit Commission for Local Authorities and the National Health Service in England and Wales.
10. *Time International*, 6.12.93.
11. Hearnden, K (1990) *A Handbook of Computer Security*.

Kogan Page, London.

12. Audit Commission (1990) *Survey of Computer Fraud and Abuse.* The Audit Commission for Local Authorities and the National Health Service in England and Wales.

13. Aken, JE (1978) *On the Control of Complex Industrial Organisations.* Nijhoff, Leiden. As cited in Hertog, FD and Wielinga, C (1992) 'Control systems in dissonance: the computer as an ink blot'. *Accounting, Organisations and Society,* 17(2), 103–127.

14. *Time International,* 6.12.93.

15. There are different kinds of block ciphers. Prominent among these is the Data Encryption Standard (DES) and FEAL-N. DES is a world-wide standard which was first adopted by the US, while FEAL-N was proposed by the Nippon Telegraph and Telephone Corporation.

16. Parker, D (1991) 'Seventeen information security myths debunked'. In Dittrich, K, Rautakivi, S and Saari, J (eds). 'Proceedings of the Sixth IFIP International Conference on Computer Security and Information Integrity in our Changing World, pp363–70). North Holland, Amsterdam.

17. Parker, D (1991) 'Seventeen information security myths debunked'. In Dittrich, K, Rautakivi, S and Saari, J (eds). 'Proceedings of the Sixth IFIP International Conference on Computer Security and Information Integrity in our Changing World, pp363–70. North Holland, Amsterdam.

18. Strain, I (1991) 'Top bosses pose the main security threat'. *Computer Weekly,* October 3, p22.

19. List, W (1993) 'IT security and the user'. *Computer Bulletin,* October, pp8–9.

20. European Commission (1994) *Green Paper on Security of Information Systems.* Draft. 4.2.1.

SERVING SOLUTIONS

COMPLIANCE
PROCEDURES

DERIVATIVES

RISK MANAGEMENT

FINANCIAL
REGULATION

BACK OFFICE
SYSTEMS

MONEY LAUNDERING

**THE CONSULTANCY AND
PROJECT MANAGERS FOR
FINANCIAL COMPLIANCE
AND REGULATION**

COMPLIANCE CONTROL LIMITED

3 College Hill
London EC4R 2RA
Tel: 44 (0) 171 626 2000
Fax: 44 (0) 171 827 0999

1.4
An International Overview of the Incidence of Economic Crime

Rowan Bosworth-Davies and Graham Saltmarsh

Economic crime has come to be regarded as a high-reward and comparatively low-risk criminal activity. The phenomenal profits that can be generated from economic crime and the rather unlikely possibility of effective law-enforcement action, renders such activity highly attractive, to those with a less than a whole-hearted commitment to the values which we normally extol in society. [1]

A barrier-free Europe now stands in more danger from the threat of organised crime than at any time in its history. As the legitimate market develops, so the 'crime enterprises' in the illegitimate market, its *alter ego*, will develop with it. No diagnosis of the extent of economic crime within the European body-politic could be complete without a full examination of the body-economic and the extent to which organised economic crime has become endemic within the commercial infrastructure. As a starting point, we should determine exactly what is meant by 'organised crime', or what the authors prefer to refer to as 'enterprise crime'.

The phrase 'enterprise crime ' can be defined as: 'the planned committing of offences for profit or to acquire power, which offences are each or together of major significance and are carried out by two or more persons who form a durable cooperation with a division of labour, using commercial-like structures, violence or the threat of it, or abusing political or public influence'.[2] This merely reflects the practical reality that organised economic crime is merely one type of entrepreneurial activity among many. Market entrepreneurs and criminal entrepreneurs are both 'market oriented'. 'They do not think in terms of national jurisdictions but in terms of flows of goods and money and in terms of the social networks of people they can trust.'[3]

The German police have a similar definition:

> The planned commission of criminal offences, determined by the pursuit of profit and power, which, individually or as a whole, are of considerable importance whenever more than two persons involved collaborate for a prolonged or indefinite period of time, each with their own appointed tasks; by using commercial or business-like structures; by using violence or by other means suitable for intimidation or by exerting influence on politics, the media, public administration, judicial authorities or the economy.[4]

The concept of the 'continuing criminal enterprise' is well entrenched elsewhere in criminological literature, with the use of the word 'enterprise' being used to identify a wide-ranging series of financially profitable activities, or as NCIS has defined them: 'a group of criminal associates whose sole purposes and loyalty is that of large-scale profit by criminal acts': as opposed to a single criminal act. Therefore, as Rider has argued, 'continuity in the activity from which these individuals seek to achieve profit is the primary characteristic of organised crime.'[5]

Organised crime corrodes the social fabric of those societies within which it is allowed to take a firm hold, because it corrupts the social infrastructures, the politicians, the police, the judiciary, and the financial institutions, for its own exclusive benefit, to such an extent that its 'pervasive influence on the politico-economic structure renders it a potential form of government'.[6] It succeeds precisely because of its essential ordinariness and because the deliberately low-profile and 'bourgeois' nature of so many of its activities tends to reflect the same capitalist aspirations and thus mirror the legitimate activities of ordinary commercial enterprises, a classic restatement of the free market paradox.

Within its own social milieu, one of the most obvious manifestations of organised crime is its absolute power; and the effect upon those whom it is able to influence, whether socially, commercially or politically, is to corrupt them absolutely. One of the identifying phenomena of organised crime is the ease with which it is able to infiltrate and corrupt the political and judicial systems of the host nation, while at the same time their activities 'can transcend national boundaries',[7] reaching to the highest positions in public life. The revelations of the alleged Mafia associations which have surrounded former Prime Minister Giulio Andreotti and the Christian Democratic Party in Italy provide ample evidence. Once achieved, such infiltration guarantees protection for the criminal enterprise and the financial interests of those who benefit by its operation, by encouraging the deliberate perception in the minds of those best placed to influence legislative change that expressions of public concern at the existence of organised crime are unecessarily alarmist, politically misguided, or socially uninformed.

The second element which has to be incorporated in creating a definition of organised crime is the recognition of the degree to which its particular commercial activities adopt the methods of and operate in similar ways to ordinary commercial practice. The third aspect which identifies an organised criminal enterprise is its clear hierarchical structure, but even this aspect can be misleading. It is distinguished from the ordinary pyramidal, commercial chain of command which exists within corporations by the added concept of the 'familial' nature of the ties within the criminal group, implying an even greater degree of loyalty, thus 'constituting a form of disciplined, self-perpetuating criminal structure.'[8]

However, the fourth aspect which clearly differentiates organised criminal commercial activity from legitimate activity is the degree of willingness for the criminal milieu to resort to acts of murder, extreme violence or the threat of such violence, and other crimes against the person. The purpose of this is to enforce 'internal discipline and to achieve passive acceptance of its activities by sections of the general population',[9] payment of its debts, to protect its investments, or to maintain the independency of its operatives, in circumstances where legitimate enterprises would be more likely to resort to formal legal action.

Bearing these four different elements in mind, it is of considerable interest, therefore, to examine the Italian legal definition of any organisation 'of a Mafia kind', which comprises:

Three or more members who make use of the power of intimidation provided by the associative bond and of the state of subjugation and of criminal silence which derives from it, to commit crimes, to acquire directly or indirectly the running or control of economic activities, of concessions, grants, contracts and public services in order to realise illicit profits or advantages for themselves or others.

In terms of the rich pickings available for organised criminal groups, the financing of the European Union provides a varied range of resources from which to squeeze illicit profits. In 1993, the official figures of losses through fraud were put at Ecu343 million (£264 million).

Commission staff admit the amount of fraud is higher than the published figure, but say the full extent is impossible to assess accurately. According to the Commission's anti-fraud unit, EU frauds worth Ecu976m were reported between 1990 and 1993. Of this, nearly half – Ecu446m – involved funds spent in Italy. Germany accounted for Ecu204m, France Ecu97m, Britain Ecu85m, Belgium Ecu32m, Greece Ecu29m, and the Netherlands Ecu25m'.[10]

One of the reasons given for the proliferation of reported Euro-fraud is the degree of complexity which surrounds the administration of the payment of subsidies. This high level of bureaucracy encourages false claims because of the inevitability that administrators will take the line of least resistance when confronted with complex claim documentation which gives all the appearances of having been completed correctly, and will sign it off in order to be able to concentrate on other, more pressing problems. Another contributing element to the incidence of fraudulent claims is the level of positive disincentive to the reporting of fraud because of the need to obtain the necessary funding for poor areas, whether by fair means or foul.

Nevertheless, the widely held perception within the European Union is that fraud is most widely practised in those countries where organised crime is most deeply entrenched. In itself, this factor offers no surprises; organised crime is always looking for new ways of acquiring access to fresh sources of financing because of its overriding need to provide itself with the means to launder its illicit profits from narcotics trafficking and other criminal enterprises. False claims for non-existent commodities have netted Southern Italian gangs in excess of Ecu20 million, while mafiosi in major Italian cities have claimed over Ecu22 million for organising training programmes which never took place. False refund claims based upon forged export documentation are rife, while frozen and deeply refrigerated products, particularly meat carcasses because of their lengthy shelf-life, can be cross-transported through a number of jurisdictions, thus obtaining maximised subsidy refund claims, while retaining a viable product which can be made available for sale, if necessary. Similar scams can be operated in the case of processed foods for which a legitimate period of time may remain until the sell by date. Other frauds involve the simple switching of labels, indicating a higher grade of product which is eligible for a higher rate of subsidy, while intervention payments, designed to encourage the depletion of food mountains, have been used to fund wholly false claims for commodities which it is claimed have been exported to Eastern European markets, when the raw material never existed in the first place.

Organised crime and the banking and financial sector are an integral part of each other's coexistence, they have always enjoyed a symbiotic relationship. This has long been true of America and Europe, but it is only relatively recently that we in the West have begun to identify just how true it is in Russia. A recent Home Office memorandum to the House of Commons Home Affairs Select Committee, which is conducting an inquiry into organised crime in Britain, has identified the surge in organised criminal activity from Russia and other East European countries. In particular, the report has singled out as being of particular concern, 'The most significant development in this context is the transfer through our financial institutions of large sums of money emanating from Central and Eastern Europe as a result of crime and clandestine activity'.

Banking services in Russia are still cast in the mould created for them by the former communist regime, which used them primarily as a means of channelling subsidised funding in the guise of 'loans' to state companies. Despite the increasing policy of privatisation, the majority shareholders in many Russian banks are still the state industries. This produces a tendency for them to be viewed as quasi 'Treasury' facilities by their managers, leading in turn to subtle, and in some cases not so subtle, pressure on bank supervisors to provide commercial facilities to the host business and its related entities, in imprudent and non-commercial circumstances. This tendency to provide lending for political as opposed to purely commercial purposes has its roots partly in the prevailing attitudes of many former communist bank officials, who are reluctant to employ prudent liquidation and bankruptcy procedures in circumstances where they would normally be indicated, but who will continue to extend credit inefficiently, thus building up an increased level of unrepayable debt.

The effect of this political influence permeates the whole of the Russian banking system, spreading outwards from the Central Bank. The latter is much criticised, not only by forward-looking Russian economists but also by the World Bank, which recently reported that at present only 20–30 Russian commercial banks are developing into recognisable banking institutions, although not even all of these are managing to reduce their exposure to institutionalised borrowers and owner–shareholders. The World Bank's report claims that central bank funds are identified and allocated 'in a manner that reflects the recipient's bargaining and political power, not on economic or financial considerations.' This concentration of patronage is perceived to be delaying effective commercial adjustment and the World Bank is adamant that the practice of the Central Bank making what it calls 'selective loans' should be abolished. In many cases, such loans are dependent upon the receipt by responsible officials of sizeable bribes, which may go some way to explain the limited number of banks who are regular recipients of these credits, a policy which causes deep resentment among non-recipient bankers. The World Bank has also identified that 'lending under these programmes does not require activities commonly linked to bank lending, like raising deposits and credit assessment.'

Another problem was that until February 1994, it was only too easy to start a bank in Russia; the minimum capital requirement was RB100 million, approximately $65,000, a figure which itself was being constantly devalued in real terms by inflation running at 20 per cent per month. The words of Dimitry Tulin, the deputy governor of the central bank possess a chilling irony when in the same month he said, 'A situation where entrepreneurs face the choice of either buying a good car or setting up a bank is paradoxical and abnormal.' Is it any wonder, therefore, that Russia has had over 2000 institutions calling themselves banks?

The regulatory, compliance and accounting standards which had traditionally applied in Russian banking procedures came nowhere near contemporary Western standards of bank auditing, making it extremely difficult to provide adequate provisioning facilities or to identify contingent liability requirements. Indeed, hitherto Russian accounting rules merely reflected that an audit had been prepared in compliance with current regulations; the true and fair opinion standard was not apparently applicable. In addition, Russian disclosure requirements have been very slack, leading to a lack of transparency in the net position of credits and liabilities among banks; coupled with a general lack of information on the identity of the bank's shareholders.

Now, very late in the day, a period of limited reform has been introduced and the Central Bank has begun to close some of the more unsound banking institutions – 21 have been closed in 1993–94, after they failed to refinance overdrafts which they had previously been financing with cheap Central Bank loans. Similarly, minimum capital requirements for new banks were raised to Rb2 billion in February 1994, although existing banks have been granted an extension until January 1995 to increase their capital. Even this increase, however, is not generally considered to pose too great a problem for the most outrageous of the mafia-controlled banks, whose funding will simply be increased by their criminal managers to comply with the new regulations and then later withdrawn at an opportune moment. To try to minimise the risk still posed, the permitted minimum capital adequacy requirement is intended to rise to the EU threshold of Ecu5 million by 1999. In October 1993 new bank financial reporting provisions were introduced, but, as Mikhail Kislyakov, a representative of Arthur Andersen, identified in March 1994, 'there are still no regulations on how banks should cover the capital part of their balance sheet by offsetting loan risk with liquid, secure assets.'

All these aspects illustrate the crisis in the Russian banking system, a state of affairs which is being openly exploited by the organised criminals and which poses considerable risks to Western banking systems, business and law enforcement. Without an effective, secure banking system, Russia can not hope to create the sophisticated financial interface with the rest of the free-market economy which it needs to develop and expand; nor does the present level of available administrative expertise and the continued use of the banking system for criminal purposes hold out much hope for the immediate future. The same is generally true of the privatisation programme as a whole, despite the apparent efficient speed with which it has been effected. A large percentage of the free vouchers (intended to become shares) which were dispensed to 40 million Russian workers, managers and to the public quickly found their way into the hands of organised ciminals. David Roche of investment bankers Morgan Stanley has estimated that between 70–80 per cent of the priva-tised industries and commercial banks are paying regular commis-sions to organised criminal groups, effectively extinguishing any potential profit which might be capable of being generated. The programmes designed to facilitate the creation of effective finan-cial exchanges are fraught with bureaucratic obstruction. Kenneth Clarke, the British Chancellor of the Exchequer, at a G7 meeting in Washington in April was forced to spell out to the Russian delegation the risks involved in hindering the process of reform. The reform programme for the development of a securities market is in a state of flux, if for no other reason that no one within the system can agree who is in overall charge of the privatisation programme. A conference in Moscow in April to debate the problem saw regional representatives accusing Moscow of monopolising the privatisation process; while Moscovite prac-titioners insisted that the blame should be placed firmly at the door of the Central Bank, which, with its half a dozen separate computer systems, none compatible with the others, is respon-sible for the failure to modernise Russia's struggling settlements system. The fledgling Securities Exchange Commission is attempting to create a unified system of commonly recognised, self-regulated dealing rules, but in a country which has over 80 stock exchanges spanning 11 time zones and regulated in a piecemeal fashion by competing state entities, it comes as little surprise that investors have discovered to their costs that these markets are riddled with fraud. Jonathan Hay, an adviser to the Securities Commission, is reported as saying, 'There are so many fake shares out there, in addition to all the scandals we have. Some funds are just selling air. If the public gets the wrong idea, this could stop the whole privatisation process.'

It may be thought paradoxical and perhaps not particularly helpful to offer a British view of fraud and criminality within the Russian banking infrastructure, but in addition to our own professional experiences on behalf of clients who have discovered, the hard way, what doing business in Russia means, the reports of professional colleagues and expert practitioners within the Russian law enforcement environment provide ample proof of the scale of the corruption within the system. Alexei Belov, deputy head of the interior ministry's criminal investigation department, reported in March, 'A big proportion of our banks are linked to mafia and criminal gangs, and are involved with money laundering. The Italian mafia is like a kindergarten compared to our Russian mafia.' The deputy head of currency control at the Central Bank, Vladimir Smirnov, goes further: 'We know that some banks employ former convicts and criminals who have spent time in jail. But it is not up to the Central Bank to deal with this sort of problem'. That may well have been Mr Smirnov's position in March 1994, but if the Central Bank does not take steps to identify whose responsibility it is to determine fitness and proper procedures for bank employees, then the existing situation will merely continue to deteriorate. Part of the problem, however, is that there are positive disincentives for administrators to involve themselves too openly in the banking system, because banking has become a very high-risk business in Russia.

Organised crime has infiltrated the banks to such a degree that introducing financial prudency procedures has now literally become a matter of life or death. In 1993, in Moscow alone, more than 12 Russian senior financiers were assassinated; to date none of the murders has been solved. Elsewhere in Russia, another 18 bankers were killed, together with 94 other people described in the police crime reports as 'entrepreneurs'. A senior

interior ministry official, Aleksandr Gurov, identified the scale
of the problem earlier in 1994 when he referred to the level of
criminal infiltration of the Russian banking system. Speaking to
foreign observers at a conference on organised crime, he talked
about the ways in which the Russian Mafia had taken over large
sectors of the financial system. He singled out for particular
comment the level of research undertaken by the gang leaders
to provide themselves with detailed knowledge of the activities
and movements of senior financial executives. Bankers who
refused to provide low-interest loans for mafia-linked business
projects; or to launder cash through their institutions to accounts
held outside Russia; or who were merely reluctant to pay the
protection demands being made on them, were singled out for
assassination.

Boris Yakubovich, the manager of Inkombank in St Petersburg,
was killed as he left for work in July 1993. Earlier in 1993,
Vladimir Rovensky, the vice-chairman of Tekhombank, was shot
down on his own doorstep. In December, Nikolai Likhachev,
chairman of Rosselkhozbank, an agricultural financing bank,
who had refused to pay extortion money to a mafia group, was
shot dead between his front door and his armoured limousine.
When $2,000 will hire a competent hit man in Moscow or St
Petersburg, merely beating up unwilling bank managers is no
longer considered to be a practical option. General Mikhail
Yegorov, chief of Russian law enforcement, puts it this way,
'They know where to find you, they make it their business to
know your business and they do not find that "no" is an acceptable answer.'

Part of the problem associated with the generalised activities
of the mafias is that, to many Russian men and women in the
street, the present criminal mafia is merely an extension of organised criminal-style structures which existed under the old communist regime. To the ordinary Russian citizen, it does not really
matter whether the present wise guys are Chechen gangsters or
former KGB operatives, the practical reality is that nothing has
really changed. This degree of resigned cynicism has spilled over
to other areas of law enforcement, and there is a perception that
one of the reasons for the failure to investigate these crimes effectively stems from the cultural disinclination for many old-style

police supervisors to demonstrate a high degree of sympathy for bankers and entrepreneurs. To many former communist apparatchiks, banking and related financial practices are still looked upon as merely another form of capitalist exploitation, and the commercial lending of money is thought to be an unsavoury business which tends to attract the criminogenic element. Boris Kondrashev, deputy head of the Moscow police department, is reported as saying, 'Many financiers bring these problems on themselves. They get involved with the mafia and end up very dead. Once their toe is in the mafia trap, they are lost forever.'

As an active detective and a former detective, we do not find it hard to sympathise with the police in one sense. They are wholly overwhelmed with the immediate logistical problems of dealing with their day-to-day criminal problems, which to Western eyes appear insurmountable. In February 1994, General Yegorov identified in excess of 40,000 commercial enterprises which he stated were wholly controlled by organised crime. He also referred, almost as if in passing, to the average investigations undertaken by police each month: over 700 allegations of extortion and racketeering; 15 of kidnapping and hostage taking; and 35 armed clashes between rival gangs. These figures were extrapolated from criminal statistics which record a reported murder rate of 25,000 victims a year, and which identified 20,000 crimes a year alone involving the use of firearms. When crime is occurring at this sort of rate, paying protection money to the gangsters is a merely another way of doing business. It has been estimated that 80 per cent of all businesses in Russia pay some form of tribute – anywhere between 10–20 per cent of gross revenues – to the mafias, a set of figures which gears consumer prices upwards by anything between 20–30 per cent more than they would normally be.

Faced with statistics like these, it is perhaps not surprising that the police view with distaste bankers who have been willing to undertake business dealings with the mafia while it suited them, but cry out when the going gets tougher and the gangs start to call in the favours. Nevertheless, the level of organised criminal activity does cause grave concern to informed observers. In February 1994, the Russian Analytical Centre for Social and Economic Policies reported the problem in these words, 'The growth of organised crime threatens the continued political and economic development of Russia and creates conditions that could help bring national socialists to power.'

An associated problem for those in the West trying to understand what this level of criminality means in real terms is that the very use of phrases such as 'organised crime' or 'mafia' has very little practical reality, because of the inevitable tendency to perceive these groups, wrongly, as somehow sharing a similar ethnic or subcultural identification as the classic Italian–American image of the 'wise guy'. Russian organised criminals, while there are a growing number of reports of their having had 'sit-downs' with US and Italian gangsters to identify areas of mutually profitable interest, do not share the same characteristics. Their freedom to operate is as much to do with the present broadly lawless state of the CIS, a situation described by Paddy Rawlinson of the London School of Economics as 'a country in a state of anomie', as any generalised but abstract concept of a hierarchical, continuing criminal enterprise.

Among their many organised criminal enterprises, money laundering within and through the Russian banking system is construed as being of particular concern to the law enforcement authorities. Andrei Ilyinsky, chief dealer at Moscow's commercial Imperial Bank, described the situation in this way, 'Many banks we see in the market today are money-laundering institutions and have nothing to do with banking. They are here today, gone tomorrow.' The greatest problem is that so many of these banks have been merely a financial conduit for their organised criminal owners, lending money to related criminal entities at wholly non-commercial rates, and then accessing cheap credits from the central bank to finance their lending policies. The present level of illegal currency transactions between criminal sources in the hard-currency West and the criminal sources inside Russia is already causing considerable alarm to banking analysts, and the banks themselves do not appear to possess the necessary degree of security to prevent abuse. A recent report in *Futures and Options World* noted:

Of the Russian money that banks gain in their day-to-day operations, part goes to pay wages, part is creamed off by corrupt bankers and ends up in private hands, and part is shipped overseas as dollars bought at hard-currency exchanges. Very little is used as investment capital . . . an investor's money could disappear in the three–four days it takes him to convert his roubles to US dollars or DM.

Swapping roubles for other forms of Western currency may seem like a pointless commercial exercise; but when the currency is 'crack' cocaine the roubles can be used to acquire Russian assets, which in turn can buy immense power inside Russia. As long ago as 1992, Georgij Mathukin, the president of the Bank of Russia, reported that over $200 million worth of roubles had been illegally exported from Russia by Western criminal syndicates; while at the same time, investigators in Italy were listening into telephone conversations between organised crime gangs in Milan who were discussing whether to credit the roubles they had illicitly acquired in Moscow or Zurich.

In 1993, in a series of desperate attempts to stabilise the economic situation and to arrest the illicit rouble exchange mechanism, the Russians engineered a widespread banknote exchange programme as one step in a wider attempt to introduce much needed monetary and financial reforms. Later in the year, but as part of the same reform programme, banks who appeared to be reluctant to implement lending-prudency provisions, and who were themselves 'overdrawn' in relation to the Central Bank as a result of indisciplined lending policies, or worse still unrepaid borrowings made by organised criminal elements, found themselves faced with interest rates of 420 per cent, coupled with severe limitations on the volume of funds such banks could borrow to finance present overdraft facilities. Much of the impetus for these reforms stemmed from the requirements of the International Monetary Fund, which had insisted on positive evidence of concerted action by the Central Bank to control the money supply and to prevent undercapitalised banking institutions being used merely as conduits for syphoning money out of Russia to secret accounts in Switzerland, Luxembourg and Liechtenstein, before it would agree to the provision of a $1.5 billion IMF loan, which had been put on hold pending the implementation of reforms.

Illicitly moving money abroad in the form of dollar-based capital flight presents particular problems for bank supervisors. This has stemmed in part from the new commercial freedoms enjoyed in post-communist Russia and the decentralisation of the economy. Under the old system, exports and imports could be controlled more rigidly and all settlements were effected through the Soviet Vneshekonombank, which could oversee the limited number of commercial agencies through which most foreign trade deals were organised. The new Federal Currency and Export Control Service is now responsible for maintaining surveillance on the movements of currency. Its deputy head, Aleksandr Sedov, has identified how the development of a market economy has resulted in a dramatic increase in the number of entities engaging in foreign commercial activity. He singles out the number of banks, in excess of 800, which have been granted the right to carry out currency transactions, identifying their activities as having cost Russia an estimated $40 billion in capital flight.

Part of the problem stems from the fact that, following perestroika, there was a general relaxation of the rules dealing with the acceptance of foreign currencies, leading to a greater drift towards reliance on the stable US dollar in preference to the rouble. At the beginning of 1993 one US dollar was worth 570 roubles. In January 1994 it was being exchanged for 1270 roubles. Following a Central Bank decree announced in October 1993, cash sales for dollars and other convertable currencies have been banned. The move, which is intended to stabilise the rouble, is also intended to help to undermine organised crime, according to Yevgeny Ivanov, head of the Central Bank's hard currency control department. 'The measure may not do much in terms of strengthening the Rouble, but it will certainly make money laundering more complicated for illegal businesses.' Many other commentators believe his words merely represent a triumph of hope over experience.

Money-laundering techniques presently being adopted by Russian criminals make considerable use of foreign banks and commercial entities which appear to be only too willing to facilitate the handling of very large sums of cash while maintaining total discretion over the sources of the money. British conference organisers have discovered a rich vein of Russian money which is available to be spent on attending technical conferences and seminars in London. Many of them have found that the conferences they organise are heavily oversubscribed by potential Russian delegates who are more than willing to pay the fees demanded, but who spend little or no time in the conference hall when they arrive. These companies have themselves inadvertently become part of the capital-flight infrastructure, because one of the side benefits for Russians of attending such conferences is a temporary entry visa to the United Kingdom; once there, the delegates are free to spend their time arranging their business affairs, activities which the National Criminal Intelligence Service presently estimates to have introduced in excess of \$19 billion to the London financial sector.

Elsewhere in former communist states, economic crime is being increasingly targeted as a significant cause of concern, although the extent to which publicly stated expressions of intent and high-flown policy statements are matched in practice with additional resource allocation is difficult to quantify. In Georgia, for instance, a decree for dealing with economic crime issued in October 1993 stated:

> Corruption, and the criminal activities of mafiosi structures have reached unprecedented dimensions. . . . [The fight against these forces will] assist the development of a market economy, create suitable conditions for the development of business in every sphere of the economy and support the implementation of radical economic reforms.

Similarly in Kyrgyzstan, the country's president, Askar Akayev, addressed a law enforcement seminar in October 1993 during which he identified the need to establish law and order throughout the republic as being an issue of vital importance. He said, 'The time has come for taking decisive steps toward protecting the lives of our citizens and creating suitable conditions for the implementation of economic reforms.' He singled out the need to control the illegal stockpiling of arms for the purposes of arms trafficking; and the auditing of all recently privatised property to tackle what he identified as widespread tax evasion in commercial life.

In the Czech Republic, the adoption of a market economy has fuelled an explosion in economic criminality as criminal entrepreneurs exploit the financial possibilities now available to them. New technology has provided the Czech fraudsters with fresh areas of enterprise, with video piracy now controlling approximately half the entire video market, a black economy worth in excess of 1 billion Czech Crowns ($34 million) annually. Weeks before the film *Jurassic Park* opened officially in Czech cinemas, the newspapers were advertising pirated video copies for sale.

The police recognise that the level of reported white-collar crime represents literally the tip of the criminal iceberg. In October 1993, a computer fraud case illustrated how exposed the Czech financial institutions were to subversion and illicit infiltration. Martin Janku, a young employee of Ceska Sporitelna, the largest Czech savings bank, stood trial, charged with stealing 35 million Czech Crowns ($1.19 million) from various accounts within the bank, and transferring the money to his own account. He was accused of cracking into the bank's transfer system on 32 separate occasions, using a software program he had written to circumvent the electronic security systems. His activities were not discovered by the computer systems or the bank's management. Despite his defence that he had committed the offences in order to illustrate the bank's vulnerability to subversion, he had considerable difficulty in explaining how it was he was caught stuffing cash into a briefcase by the police, they having been alerted to his activities by the bank cashier when Janku withdrew 15 million Crowns ($508,100) over the counter.

In the face of rising criminal statistics, the Hungarian government has approved a coordinating committee to fight economic crime. The committee includes members of the national authorities responsible for economic administration, the police fraud squad and the office of Customs and Excise. Also included will be the chief public prosecutor, the National Bank president and the president of the State Audit Office.

The former Eastern bloc countries are not without help from the West in the creation of their crime prevention programmes. At an international conference held in Sinaia, Romania in May 1994, representatives from Interpol pledged assistance to their police colleagues in East Europe and the former Soviet Union. Recognising the importance of Eastern European countries as transit routes for the movement of heroin from the Far East into Western Europe, the conference discussed ways to deal with organised criminal activity, including the developing links between criminal gangs in the East with their counterparts in the West.

Elsewhere in the world, economic crime remains the main source of criminal concern for regulators and law enforcement bodies. In Malaysia, reports of commercial crime rose by over 300 per cent in ten years, but even these figures were estimated to represent only 15 per cent of the real incidence of fraud. 'The terms, "white collar crime", "commercial crime", and "economic crime", are generally used to refer to offences such as corporate or securities fraud, share market manipulation, insider trading, currency counterfeiting, loan sharking, bribery and corruption.'[11] Other developing forms of economic criminality, such as extortion and consumer terrorism, were identified by Dr Barry Rider of Jesus College, Cambridge in a paper to the International Symposium on Economic Crime held in Kuala Lumpur in March 1994:

> Extortion has become a work of art in some countries ... extortionists have become more sophisticated, particularly in terms of using banks in different countries to move the money until it can not be traced ... organised crime especially, have a lot of experience in money laundering and are looking for ways to invest money in legitimate businesses.

Economic crime is reported to be costing Australia in excess of $12 billion annually. The Insurance Council of Australia has calculated that fraudulent insurance claims will amount to $1.7 billion annually, broken down into $620 million for fraudulent worker's compensation claims; $800 million for false motor insurance claims; $100 million for bogus household claims; and a mere $62 million for fires. Public sector fraud, on the other hand, includes $3 billion for tax frauds; $2 billion for social security fiddles; $2.5 billion for Customs and Excise avoidance; $800 million for defence scams; and $700 million for health rip-offs. Other growth areas for fraud included state and private sector pension schemes which, it is estmated, will be reporting losses in excess of $300 billion by the year 2000, while advance-fee frauds are now utilising the resource time of a uniquely tasked strike force.[12]

In communist China, a report published in March 1994 by the State Administration for Industry and Commerce reported that in excess of 150,000 cases of criminal infractions of the economic laws and regulations were undertaken in the previous year, of which 30,000 were described as being 'major or serious'. A large percentage of this reported criminal activity involved state-owned or collective units, and the largest increase in economic criminal cases was identified in the area of product counterfeiting and smuggling. Interestingly, new forms of illicit business enterprises appeared, including foreign-exchange speculation on the black market, customers being apparently gulled into parting with their money on the promise of 'high investment returns in futures trading'.

Turning Westward, insurance fraud has been identified as becoming a 'nationwide epidemic' in the US.

> The nature of the insurance business makes it susceptible to fraud because it is a risk distribution system driven by a constant demand for insurance products. This demand creates a steady flow of cash that must be accumulated in liquid reserves in order to pay claims.[13]

This has been described as a 'special emphasis area' by the Economic Crime Council, a federal law enforcement body with special responsibility for economic crimes. So acute has the crisis become that specialist task-forces have been set up comprising teams of investigators drawn from the FBI, the Internal Revenue Service, the US Postal Inspector's Department and lawyers from the respective US Attorney's departments.

The regulation of the US insurance industry has been high on the law enforcement agenda since 1991 when the US Senate's Permanent Subcommittee on Investigations looked into the regulation of insurance fraud. It has recently received an added incentive by the re-emergence of 'Savings and Loans' scams, where a number of infamous S&L rip-offs have been linked to real-estate transactions of dubious worth, one method being the deliberate inflation of real-estate projects coupled with worthless lending schemes which are being used to syphon off insurance capital reserves. Using a company's liquid capital to purchase heavily overvalued real estate gives the impression that the company has increased its invested asset value, and can be used to deceive the regulators into thinking that its liquidity ratios are being maintained when in fact the money is being quietly redistributed elsewhere.

> Insurance fraud is particularly difficult to investigate because of the complex regulatory framework, sophisticated schemes and the prevalence of con-artists. Complicating things further is the need for a forensic examination which involves an analysis of voluminous documents. Many good cases are abandoned out of frustration when an investigator gets lost or bogged down in the paper trail. Because fraudulent activity has reached national proportions, the state and federal criminal justice system must act as a safety net for the public. Aggressive prosecution is the only language that con-artists understand. Unfortunately, the criminal justice system is slow to react and rarely compensates the victims.[14]

By way of summation, it is worth observing that regulation by prosecution has become an option increasingly resorted to in the armoury of American regulators and law enforcers, as there is widespread recognition of the need for a greater degree of prophylactic measures to combat the insidious effects of organised criminal fraud within the capitalist market. Perhaps the last word on the subject should be left to Robert Morgenthau, the District Attorney of Manhattan, who voiced his growing concerns over the problems caused to the social and financial infrastructure of his city by the effects of the BCCI affair.

The New York criminal investigation alleged that BCCI had systematically falsified its banking records; that it had knowingly laundered illegal drug proceeds; and that it paid bribes and dishonest commissions to public officials. In December 1991, BCCI and three associated companies pleaded guilty to six related counts in a twelve-count indictment and agreed to forfeit $550 million to the State of New York and the US Federal Government.

The authors believe, therefore, that there could be no better way to finish this section of a book which seeks to deal with the regulation and prevention of economic crime than by reviewing the activities of Robert Morgenthau, the Manhattan District Attorney, the man who led the prosecution of BCCI and its officers, and looking forward a little way into the future to see whether the expressed intentions of banking supervisors will be sufficient to meet the new criminal challenges.

In the course of his speech to the London School of Economics conference, 'Banking Supervision After BCCI', on 24 May 1993, in describing why he and his officers had been happy to accept the responsibility of investigating BCCI, Robert Morgenthau spelled out the social cost of the drug problem in the city of New York. He said:

> In New York, illegal drug use is a major cause of infant fatalities and birth defects. A recent study projected that more than 72,000 Crack-exposed babies will be born in New York City by the end of this decade. The cost of this tragedy in neo-natal special education and foster care alone is expected to be $2 billion. The human cost is incalculable. Another example of course is that illegal drugs are a primary cause of crime in New York City. In another recent study, more than 75% of people arrested in Manhattan tested positive for illegal drug use. For those charged with robbery, the figure was 90%. Drugs are also a major contributing factor in child abuse cases. In three quarters of such cases in my city, one or both parents is addicted to drugs.[15]

Mr Morgenthau then went on to outline his reasons for targeting banks. He said:

> The nexus between drugs and money means that to combat the use and damage of illegal drugs in our society, we must be as vigorous in our prosecution of rogue bankers as we are in our prosecution of street dealers . . . It would be devastating to our efforts if our battle against crime were ever to be viewed as solely a struggle against crimes committed by the poor and the underprivileged. There is no faster or more certain way to erode respect for the law – respect that ultimately must be the cornerstone for a society governed by laws – than to allow even the impression that the laws are enforced against certain groups, while others may commit crimes with impunity. If officials in the banking industry or in public life violate their special trusts, they must be brought to justice.[16]

In making this statement, Morgenthau was underlining the importance of his determined policy of infiltrating the entire financial base of those who have facilitated the international realisation of the profits from drug trafficking. In so doing, he was consciously making a direct attack on the corporate morality of a whole generation of bankers and financial practitioners. As Morgenthau himself said later in London:

> In short, we had to pursue the BCCI case because of its relationship to drug money and because of our obligation to prosecute 'crime in the suites' as well as 'crime in the streets'. Our efforts however, encountered many obstacles. Political pressure; international relations; bank regulations - in particular bank secrecy regulations - and, finally, the intricacy of the web of minstitutions and transactions spun by BCCI, all presented barriers to our investigation and prosecution of the affair.[17]

References

1. Rider, BAK (1990) 'Organised Economic Crime'. 8th International Symposium on Economic Crime, Jesus College, Cambridge.
2. Van Duyne, PC (1992) *Implications of Cross-Border Crime Risks in an Open Europe*. Ministry of Justice Briefing Paper, The Hague.
3. Van Duyne, PC (1992) *Implications of Cross-Border Crime Risks in an Open Europe*. Ministry of Justice Briefing Paper, The Hague.
4. Ratzel, MP (1993) 'Organised Crime: A Threat Assessment'. NCIS Bramshill Conference Papers.
5. Rider, BAK (1990) 'Organised Economic Crime'. 8th International Symposium on Economic Crime, Jesus College, Cambridge.
6. NCIS Briefing Paper (1993) 'An outline assessment of the threat and impact by organised/enterprise crime upon United Kingdom interests'.
7. NCIS Briefing Paper (1993) 'An outline assessment of the threat and impact by organised/enterprise crime upon United Kingdom interests'.
8. NCIS Briefing Paper (1993) 'An outline assessment of the threat and impact by organised/enterprise crime upon United Kingdom interests'.
9. NCIS Briefing Paper (1993) 'An outline assessment of the threat and impact by organised/enterprise crime upon United Kingdom

interests'.
10. *Financial Times*, 19.5.94.
11. *Business Times*, 28.9.93.
12. *Australian Financial Review*, October 1993.
13. *Business Insurance*, February 1994.
14. *Business Insurance*, October 1993.
15. Robert Morgenthau, 1993.
16. Robert Morgenthau, 1993.
17. Robert Morgenthau, 1993.

Part Two
TREATMENT

2.1
International Cooperation

Jonathan Reuvid

The increasing levels of international cooperation between national police forces and customs and excise services over the last 25 years has been matched by the efforts of government departments, legislators and judiciaries, particularly those of Member States of the European Union, the G7 Group of States, the OECD and the British Commonwealth to provide the machinery for assisting each other in the pursuit of suspected and convicted criminals, their repatriation and prosecution, and the recovery of the proceeds of their crimes. Given the disparities between domestic legislation, judicial systems, penal codes and the application of domestic law to foreign citizens, the task of harmonizing practices internationally is immensely complex and results have been mixed. However, the pace of international cooperation has quickened significantly during the last five years.

Much of the effort has been directed at the pursuit of drug trafficking offenders and the confiscation of the criminal proceeds of drug trafficking and the derivative money laundering activity described in Part One of this book. As noted elsewhere, drug-related crimes account for about 50 per cent of international crime. More recently, international mutual assistance has become focused on the laundering of the proceeds of non-drug trafficking crime and on instances of other serious economic crime such as major fraud, corruption and infringements of company law commonly associated with organised crime.

In this context, a more succinct version of the definitions of organised crime given on page 91 and 92 will serve:

Any enterprise or group of persons engaged in continuing illegal activities which has as its primary purpose the generation of profits irrespective of national boundaries.

The main thrust of the legislators' campaign to develop an international framework for the pursuit and prosecution of organised crime and the recovery of its proceeds has been in the drafting and enactment of a series of international conventions in preference to a proliferation of bilateral agreements. In each case, the drafting has been a long and sometimes painful process with individual participating States tabling formal reservations to specific articles, and delays in ratification. In all of this activity, the UK has played a leading role, as it has in the Ad Hoc Working Group on International Organised Crime of the European Union and formation of the National Criminal Intelligence Service (NCIS) as a pre-cursor of the Maastricht Treaty requirement in this area.

International conventions

Since 1990, the principal international conventions which have enhanced the ability of law enforcers to operate effectively across borders have been:

- Council of Europe Convention on Laundering, Search, Seizure and Confiscation of the Proceed of Crime (1990). The UK was the first country to ratify the Convention in September 1992. The scope of this convention extends far beyond economic crimes; it is intended to facilitate international cooperation in respect of investigation, search, seizure and confiscation of all kinds of criminal proceeds, especially those resulting from serious crimes, including drug offences, arms dealing, terrorist offences, trafficking in children and young women and other offences which generate high profits.
- European Community Directive on the prevention of the use of the financial system for money laundering, adopted by the Council of Economic and Finance Ministers in June 1991.

The laundering of money is prohibited, where it is the proceeds of drug trafficking, and Member States are permitted by the Directive to extend the scope of money laundering (as defined in Article 1 of the Directive) to the proceeds of any other criminal activity. The UK implemented the Directive early in 1994 by bringing into force its Criminal Justice Act 1993 (see below).

European Convention on Extradition (1957)
Since ratification by the UK in 1991, the extradition arrangements between the UK and Convention partners, including 13 other EC states, have been simpler. In October 1993, an order-in-council enabled the UK to ratify the relevant Chapter of the Second Protocol to the European Convention on Extradition which provides a more certain basis for extradition between Protocol signatories of those charged with fiscal (tax, duties, customs or exchange) offences. **Please refer to page 134 for note on the European Convention on Extradition (Fiscal Offences) Order 1993.**

Relevant UK domestic legislation

Specific measures of UK criminal legislation, mainly enacted since 1978, form the foundation for the UK Courts to administer the recent international conventions relating to the confiscation of criminal proceeds and money laundering, fraud, corruption and company law:

Drug Trafficking Act 1994 (DTA) [1]
Comprehensive legislation to ensure that those convicted of drug trafficking are prevented from retaining the profits of their illegal activities. The Act also made it an offence to assist another to retain the benefits of drug trafficking.

Criminal Justice (International Co-operation) Act 1990
supplements the DTOA by making it an offence to conceal or transfer the proceeds of drug trafficking, and to acquire such proceeds for no or inadequate consideration.

Criminal Justice Act 1988 [2]

contains provisions enabling the courts to confiscate the proceeds of indictable offences.

Extradition Act 1989

provides that an offence is extraditable if it attracts a sentence on indictment of 12 months' imprisonment or more in both countries.

Criminal Justice Act 1993 [3]

includes new offences of failing to report suspicions of money laundering and makes the laundering of the proceeds of non-drug trafficking crimes an offence.

Criminal Law Act 1977 and Theft Acts of 1968 and 1978 [4]

The Serious Fraud Office was set up under the first of these, responsible for investigating serious and complex fraud cases — usually those involving the loss of £5 million or more.

Prevention of Corruption Acts 1889 to 1916

The original Act made it an offence for someone corruptly to solicit, receive or agree to receive, for himself or any other person, any gift, loan, fee, reward or other advantage as an inducement to any member, officer or servant of a public body to do or not to do anything in relation to any matter in which the public body is concerned. It is similarly an offence corruptly

---

1. The relevant legislation in Scotland is the Criminal Justice (Scotland) Act 1987.
2. There are no similar powers in Scotland yet. The law on confiscation and forfeiture is being considered by the Scottish Law Commission.
3. Together with a comprehensive set of Regulations for credit and financial institutions, these new measures implement the prior European Community Directive on prevention of the use of the financial system for the purpose of money laundering.
4. Fraud is punishable under common law in Scotland. The Criminal Justice (Scotland) Act 1987 conferred powers identical to those of the SFO in England on officers nominated by the Lord Advocate.

to give, promise to offer such a gift, loan, fee, reward or other advantage.

Subsequent Acts extended the law beyond local government to other public bodies, including central government and to businesses, as well as to 'local and public authorities of all descriptions'. The 1916 Act also places the burden of proof on the defendant in the case of gifts to a Crown servant or employee or a public body by or on behalf of a person holding or seeking to obtain a contract with the Crown or a public body.

The Companies Act 1985

The Department of Trade and Industry (DTI) is responsible for the regulation of companies and the 1985 Act contains the main legislative provisions. UK companies are required to maintain records and file certain information at Companies House, including details of directors and shareholders and the company's registered office, as well as filing annual accounts. All these records are publicly available.

Banks, building societies, insurance and investment business are subject to external regulation. Other sectors are not subject to an external regulator, but the Secretary of State may authorize investigation under the Companies Act, if he considers there to be a good reason, in the event of a complaint against any company within these sectors or its officers.

International mutual legal assistance

In August 1991 the UK Central Authority for Mutual Legal Assistance in Criminal Matters published its guidelines for the operation of the principal measures and conventions summarised above. These guidelines are intended both for UK authorities responding to requests for assistance from foreign law enforcers in the pursuit of cross-border crime and criminals generally, and for foreign police forces and judicial authorities seeking to make the most effective use of UK law and the facilities available for cooperation. In terms of UK application, the scope of these guidelines is, of course, broadened by the Criminal Justice Act 1993 and the Second Protocol to the European Convention on Extradition ratified by the UK in 1993.

The guidelines, which do not affect the previously established procedures for the handling of extradition requests, were issued through the Home Office as the Department with responsibility as the UK Central Authority for Mutual Legal Assistance in Criminal Matters at C2 Division at 50 Queen Anne's Gate, London SW1H 9AT.

Main features of the United Kingdom guidelines

Responsible to the Secretary of State for the Home Department (the Home Secretary), the Home Office is responsible for interior and, together with the Attorney General and the Lord Chancellor, for criminal justice functions within England and Wales.

All mutual assistance requests to any part of the UK should be sent to the Central Authority, unless:

(a) there are appropriate International Police Organisation (Interpol) channels;
(b) they fall within the scope of memoranda of understanding, conventions or treaties;
(c) they fall within the scope of other arrangements for which other channels have been designated: for example, customs, financial and tax matters and other specialist areas where mutual assistance can be arranged independently by Departments outside the Home Office.

Examples of relevant treaties, conventions and memoranda of understanding are:

• the Naples and Nairobi Conventions' Customs Cooperation Council arrangements, for which HM Customs and Excise is designated as the appropriate channel of communication;
• the European Community customs legislation, for which HM Customs and Excise is also designated as the channel;

- the European Convention on Insider Trading, for which the Department of Trade and Industry has been designated;
- double taxation agreements and the European Community Mutual Assistance Directive (in relation to direct taxes), for which the designated channel is the Inland Revenue.

If considered necessary by an overseas authority, requests to the Central Authority may be sent through diplomatic channels, but direct communication is always preferred.

In the case of requests for privately held information or evidence made to the UK by authorities having specialist regulatory functions in respect of companies, financial services (including insider dealing), insurance or banking, similar to those undertaken by the UK authorities, the Secretary of State for Trade and Industry has powers under the Companies Act 1989 which he may exercise to assist a requesting authority.

The role of the DTI

The powers of the Secretary of State for the Department of Trade and Industry (DTI) are exercisable whether or not the DTI or any other UK authority has any interest in the results of the enquiry. The Secretary of State, or his authorised investigator, can oblige a person to answer questions put to him and may examine him on oath, requiring him to produce any documents specified by the investigator. In certain circumstances, he may also require the production of information or documents from banks.

On receipt of a request under the Criminal Justice (International Cooperation Act) 1990, the Central Authority may conclude that the powers under the Companies Act 1989 would be a more appropriate vehicle. In such cases, the request will be passed to the DTI for processing.

Use of Interpol channels

Requests concerning the service of documents, the taking of evidence from witnesses, suspects or accused persons, search and seizure and requests to seek the attendance of witnesses must be sent to the Central Authority. In cases of emergency, requests may be sent through Interpol National Central Bureau which also deals with police-to-police requests for mutual assistance.

The Interpol channel is used particularly for requests for information during preliminary investigations, such as identification enquiries or requests for lists of convictions.

As noted on page 70, the global information and intelligence communication role of Interpol is unaffected by the establishment of Europol as an EU information exchange system to combat drug traffickers initially and, subsequently, terrorism and other serious crime in the region.

Other UK and UK-related authorities

Scotland and Northern Ireland have their own criminal jurisdictions. However the relevant departments in each have assigned responsibility for the coordination of mutual assistance for the whole of the UK to the Central Authority.

Preliminary enquiries concerning the making of requests relating to Scotland in matters of the service of documents, taking evidence from witnesses, suspects or accused persons, search and seizure and requests to seek attendance of witnesses may be made directly to the Crown Office Fraud and Special Services Unit in Edinburgh, which administers mutual assistance requests on behalf of the Lord Advocate.

The Channel Islands and Isle of Man, which are Crown Dependencies, are not part of the UK. Although the Home Office, being responsible for the Islands' international relations, is in a position to make representations to them in respect of mutual assistance relations with other States, the Islands themselves have their individual legislations for executing requests.

Response to requests under multilateral and bilateral treaties and agreements

In addition to the more recent conventions and agreements under which the UK operates, it is also a party to each of the following measures of longer standing:

- European Convention on Mutual Assistance in Criminal Matters (1959);
- 1978 Additional Protocol to that Convention;
- Scheme relating to Mutual Assistance in Criminal Matters within the Commonwealth;
- United Nations Convention against the Illicit Traffic in Narcotic Drugs and Psychotropic Substances 1988 (the Vienna Convention).

The UK's ability to give mutual assistance under the Criminal Justice (International Cooperation Act) 1990 is not confined to countries covered by and party to the various agreements identified in this chapter. Although the terms of these agreements including the various UK reservations and declarations will apply where relevant, the UK does not require bilateral treaties or agreements before help may be given. However, where the legislation of another State requires a treaty before it can grant the UK full reciprocal assistance, the UK may consider entering into a bilateral agreement.

In the case of assistance requested in relation to the confiscation of criminal assets, the UK will normally require a multilateral or bilateral confiscation agreement to be in place before responding positively.

Form and content of requests

Authorities abroad which have the function of making mutual assistance requests may be courts, tribunals or examining magistrates and may include Ministries or Departments of Justice, Attorneys General and other judicial authorities.

Requests to the Central Authority must take the form of formal written requests headed 'To the Competent UK Authority'. Advance faxed copies of urgent requests (or telexed or radioed requests through Interpol) may be used to speed up execution, subject to an undertaking to forward the original request by air mail or courier promptly (usually within seven days). Instruction on the necessary information to accompany any request is detailed in Appendix I to this chapter. The original of any request in a language other than English must be accompanied by an accurate translation.

Should the assistance requested cease to be required the Central Authority or other recipient of the original request for assistance should be informed without delay.

The Criminal Justice (International Co-operation) Act 1990

As the principal source of UK mutual assistance powers, the operation in practice of the Criminal Justice (International Co-operation) Act 1990 and its limitations need to be understood.
The Act has introduced significant new powers to assist other States in the investigation and prosecution of offences:

(a) the Secretary of State or, in Scotland the Lord Advocate, is empowered to carry out the service of process on behalf of another jurisdiction;
(b) the Secretary of State (or Lord Advocate) is permitted to direct a Court to take evidence at the investigation as well as the prosecution stage of proceedings in another jurisdiction;
(c) the Secretary of State is enabled to permit persons in detention to appear as witnesses or otherwise to assist in proceedings abroad;
(d) search and seizure on behalf of another jurisdiction is permitted;
(e) provision is made for the certification of evidence where necessary.

The execution of each of these categories of action is subject to the observance of specific regulations and procedures detailed in the various sections of the Act. Although Section 7 (1) extends the powers contained in Part II of the Police and Criminal Evidence Act 1984, the regulations relating to search and seizure on behalf of another jurisdiction are particularly stringent.

Search for and seizure of evidence may be carried out in respect of either an investigation or a prosecution, in circumstances where conduct in the other jurisdiction would have constituted 'a serious arrestable offence' in the UK, a matter on which only UK courts can decide. The following is a summary of what constitutes an 'arrestable offence' in English law and of the statutory criteria for regarding any   individual arrestable offence as 'serious' for the purpose of the exercise of these powers:

- Arrestable offences are those for which the penalty is fixed by law (eg life sentences for murder and treason), offences carrying a penalty of five or more years' imprisonment and various statutory offences, including offences of indecent assault on a woman, causing prostitution of women, procuring a girl under 21, taking a motor vehicle or other conveyance without authority, going equipped for stealing and certain offences for which a person may be arrested under Customs and Excise Acts.
- Serious arrestable offences, in all circumstances, are defined to include treason, murder, manslaughter, rape, kidnapping, incest or intercourse with a girl under 13; buggery with a boy under 16 or someone who has not consented; indecent assault which amounts to gross indecency; possession of firearms with intent to injure; carrying firearms with criminal intent; use of firearms or imitation firearms to resist arrest; causing explosions likely to endanger life or property; and hostage taking, hijacking and certain offences under sections 1,9 and 10 of the Prevention of Terrorism (Temporary Provisions) Act 1984.

In addition, any other arrestable offence may be treated as 'serious' for the purpose of exercising the relevant powers, if it has led or is likely to lead to:

- Serious harm to the security of the State or public order; serious interference with the administration of justice or with the investigation of offences; the death of anyone; serious

injury to anyone; substantial financial gain or serious financial loss to any person.

The Central Authority will require sufficient information to be
provided about the offence to which the request refers and its
commission to enable a court to decide whether these criteria
have been satisfied.

Having satisfied the criteria as to the classification of the
offence, the requesting authority has then to provide a reasonable explanation as to how the evidence sought is 'likely to be
of substantial value' to the investigation, either on its own or in
conjunction with other material.

When requesting a search warrant under the 1984 Act, of
which the issue is dependent on the fact that a serious arrestable
offence has been committed, it is crucial to supply the magistrate to whom application is made with sufficient information
to conclude that the statutory criteria have been met. In addition, information necessary to satisfy the magistrate that one or
more of the following conditions has been satisfied should be
included in the request:

(i) that it is not practicable to communicate with any person
entitled to grant entry to the premises;
(ii) that while (i) may be possible, it is not practicable to communicate with any person entitled to grant access to the evidence;
(iii) that entry to the premises will not be granted unless a warrant
is produced;
(iv) that the purpose of a search may be frustrated or seriously
prejudiced unless a constable arriving at the premises can
secure immediate entry to them.

Even when the three sets of conditions described above have been
satisfied, overseas authorities may still be denied access by the
court to the material sought if it is held on a confidential basis.
UK legislation provides for varying degrees of protection,
depending on the degree of confidentiality involved (for example,
whether the material sought consists of items subject to legal privilege, represents medical or other personal records, or is simply
held on a general understanding of confidence). Items subject to

legal privilege are always outside the scope of these provisions, but other confidential information may sometimes be accessible and the Central Authority will advise the overseas authority of any further information likely to be required by the court when considering the application. Legal privilege (broadly speaking, the privilege attaching to communications between lawyer and client) does not arise where the lawyer has been involved wittingly or unwittingly in the commission of a crime.

Section 7(2) of the 1990 Act does provide some relief by extending a search power in respect of actions that would constitute a serious arrestable offence to actions that would constitute simply and arrestable offence in certain circumstances. A search warrant may be sought in respect of such offences, on the Secretary of State's authority, provided that:

(a) criminal proceedings have been instituted in respect of the overseas offence, or someone has been arrested for it;
(b) there are reasonable grounds for suspecting that there is evidence relating to the offence on the premises to be searched; and
(c) those premises are occupied or controlled by the person who has been arrested or against whom proceedings have been taken.

A request for a search warrant, with supporting information, will be entertained where the overseas authority believes that the subject matter of its request may fall into this category.

The operation of the law in Scotland is somewhat different, but Section 8 (1) of the Criminal Justice (International Co-operation) Act 1990 enables the Sheriff Court in Scotland to grant warrants authorising entry, search and seizure on the same basis as it can at common law in respect of offences punishable at common law in Scotland. Before the Sheriff can grant such a warrant he must conclude:

(a) that there are reasonable grounds for believing that an offence under the law of a country or territory outside the UK has been committed; and
(b) that the conduct constituting that offence would constitute

an offence punishable by imprisonment if it had occurred in Scotland.

Operating under common law rather than statute, the Sheriff Court will require to be satisfied, before issuing a search warrant, not only that an offence has been committed which would constitute an offence punishable by imprisonment in Scotland, but also that there are reasonable grounds for believing that evidence relating to that offence could be found on any premises to be searched.

Fiscal offences

Except for requests from Commonwealth countries and requests made pursuant to a treaty to which the UK is a party, including the European Convention on Mutual Assistance in Criminal Matters, requests for assistance in obtaining formal evidence in relation to fiscal offences will be accepted only if the activity is also a criminal offence in the UK.

Investigation of serious fraud

Under Section 2 of the Criminal Justice Act 1987, the Director of the Serious Fraud Office may investigate and prosecute any offence which, specifically in relation to England, Wales and Northern Ireland, which appears to the Director to involve serious or complex fraud.

The powers of the SFO include authority to require that a person whose affairs are under investigation, or any other person whom the Director has reason to believe is in possession of relevant information or documents, should attend and answer questions, furnish information and produce documents. In addition, there are circumstances in which a magistrate may, on the basis of the sworn deposition of a member of the SFO, issue a warrant to the police to enter premises, to search for and seize relevant documents. Normally, the Criminal Justice (International Co-operation) Act 1990 provides sufficient authority to obtain documents required for investigations or prosecutions abroad. However, the Central Authority will consult with the SFO in cases of overseas requests involving serious or complex fraud.

In Scotland, similar powers may be exercised by officers operating within the Crown Office Fraud and Specialist Service Unit, nominated by the Lord Advocate under Section 52 of the Criminal Justice (Scotland) Act 1987.

In the past two years criticism of the SFO has been plentiful, following its failure to obtain convictions in a small number of prominent fraud trials which have attracted great public interest, and whose prosecution has been conducted at great public expense. However, few suggestions have been made how the prosecution of fraud in the UK could be improved. A government review carried out in 1994 recommended that the SFO and the fraud investigation group of the Crown Prosecution Service (CPS) be merged, with overall control of the merged organisation vested in the CPS. However, a second working party report, before the attorney-general as this book goes to press, recommends that the SFO should be retained in its present form. The argument in favour of maintained SFO independence is the conflicting structures of the two organisations. The CPS was established as a purely prosecuting authority, whereas the SFO oversees both the investigation and the prosecution of cases. The present Director of the SFO has said that the organisation is too small to cope with significant fluctuations in the number of cases referred to it; the working party, which appears to have accepted this point, has been studying how much of the case load of the CPS's fraud investigation group should be taken over by the SFO.

Refusal of assistance

Instances of refusal by the UK to provide assistance are rare. Except in clear-cut cases, the Central Authority will normally consult with the requesting State to discuss how any difficulties preventing execution may be overcome, before finally deciding that a request cannot be executed, either wholly or in part.

Generally, assistance cannot be granted where execution of a request would be contrary to UK law or established practice, although refusal may be made on political, security or national interest grounds. As discussed in the Central Authorities guidelines, search and seizure may be refused if the circumstances do not satisfy the UK legislation's requirement and evidence may not be taken or passed on where a witness has made a substantiated claim to privilege. Assistance may also be refused where overseas proceedings may result in retrial for an offence for which the accused has already been tried in the UK or elsewhere (the principle of double jeopardy). Equally, the transfer of a prisoner may have to be refused if the prisoner is very near the date of release in the UK or is required for proceedings in the UK courts.

Where assistance in the service of a summons or other process is requested, the Secretary of State may take into account a number of matters, including whether it is appropriate to the public interest, before deciding whether to exercise his powers under the Companies Act 1989.

Requests from the United Kingdom

The UK Central Authority, namely the C2 Division of the Home Office, also acts as the clearing house for the checking and transmission of requests for mutual assistance from UK courts and authorities for assistance from the courts and authorities of other States. In the event that a State will not accept requests from the Central Authority, they are passed through diplomatic channels.

The UK has designated the following Law Officers and public prosecutors, in addition to its courts, as authorities competent to make mutual assistance requests:

- Attorney General for England and Wales
- Director of Public Prosecutions
- Crown Prosecutors
- Serious Fraud Office
- Investigations Division of the Department of Trade and Industry
- any Assistant Secretary (Legal) in charge of a Prosecuting Division of HM Customs and Excise Lord Advocate (Scotland)
- Procurators Fiscal (Scotland)

- Director of Public Prosecutions (Northern Ireland)
- Attorney General (Northern Ireland)

The majority of formal requests forwarded by the Central Authority relate to the obtaining of evidence for use in a prosecution, but UK requests for mutual assistance may relate to any aspect of the investigation or prosecution of offences. UK courts and the authorities listed above are authorised to make requests direct to courts or tribunals abroad in case of urgency. In some cases preliminary enquiries may have been made already through Interpol channels as a part of normal police-to-police cooperation arrangements.

Particular United Kingdom requirements

As with other jurisdictions which operate under a system of common law, hearsay evidence cannot be used normally in UK proceedings. Therefore, in many cases, applications from the UK for mutual assistance include a request that a police officer or other UK official may be present at the taking of evidence, may participate in the questioning and may be permitted to take a copy of the evidence back to the UK.

Under section 3(8) of the Criminal Justice (International Cooperation) Act 1990, a court in England and Wales has to consider:

(a) whether it was possible to challenge any witness statement taken abroad by questioning the witness; and
(b) where proceedings have been instituted, whether the local law allowed the parties to the proceedings to be legally represented when the evidence was being presented.

Authorities or courts executing a request from the UK are therefore asked to include these details in their replies. They are also asked to be informed if witnesses assert privilege under UK law, and whether evidence has been taken on oath.

Witness immunity

Immunity from prosecutions is not conferred automatically where the UK has requested the appearance of a witness or person in detention abroad to assist in proceedings in the UK. The granting of immunity will be considered carefully, only when it is specifically requested by the person to whom it would apply or by the authorities of the country from whom assistance is requested. The UK will not grant immunity where this would be contrary to the public interest.

European Ad Hoc Working Group on Organised Crime

The main conclusions of the Ad Hoc Working Group on Organised Crime of the European Union are set out below in terms of recommendations for action by individual Member States and collective action. The UK position on each of the recommended individual actions is summarized under each heading.

Action by individual Member States

- provision of legal sanctions against legal persons (already provided for under UK law);
- ratification of 1990 Council of Europe Convention on Laundering, Search, Seizure and Confiscation of the Proceeds of Crime (Convention ratified by the UK in 1992);
- adoption of measures to allow for the confiscation of proceeds derived from offences irrespective of conviction of the perpetrators (UK can enforce overseas in rem forfeiture orders in respect of drug trafficking and serious crime where there has not been a criminal conviction.);
- adoption of long time limits for prosecution of criminal offences relating to international organised crime (time limits on prosecutions in the UK do not apply to indictable offences);
- obligations to report money laundering offences and suspicious transactions should apply more widely than to drug traf-

ficking (The 1993 Criminal Justice Act extends main money laundering provisions to serious crime other than drug trafficking).

Recommended collective action

- Development and regular updating of networks of national contact points on police/customs cooperation and judicial cooperation set up by the Ad Hoc Working Group;
  (The UK contact points are the National Criminal Intelligence Service on police/customs cooperation and the Home Office on judicial cooperation)
- an annual report to be made to EC Interior and Justice Ministers concerning the scale and trends of organised crime;
- regular exchange of information on the provisions and effectiveness of national laws relating to organised crime;
- continuing study of the scope to simplify the legal arrangements for judicial cooperation between Member States to overcome difficulties associated with differences in national laws, such as offence definition and prosecution time limits;
- in relation to money laundering, further study of the desirability and practicability of applying the obligation to report suspicious transactions (currently applicable to financial institutions) to other relevant professions and organisations; also work to improve cooperation between the 12 members of the EU in respect of the sharing of information derived from disclosures;
- exchange of experience and information about witness protection methods and consideration of effective measures to protect other persons (eg jury members) involved in the administration of justice.

Confiscation

As we have seen already both international conventions and domestic legislation relating to confiscation of the illegal proceeds of serious crime overall have their origin in measures designed to stop drug traffickers from being able to retain and use the proceeds of their criminal activities. Thus a key element in concerted national and international anti-drugs strategy is to deny to criminals the huge profits derived from the drugs trade in the form of laundered money.

The aims of measures authorising the confiscation of laundered money are:

(a) deterrent – making drug trafficking less profitable;
(b) preventive – stopping the reinvestment of the proceeds in further criminal activities, drug trafficking or otherwise;
(c) investigative – enabling investigators to follow the money t rail, thereby making it easier to identify and dismantle criminal organisations.

The same set of arguments applies with similar force to the proceeds of criminal conduct generally and is recognised in the UK Criminal Justice Act 1993 which extends the power of confiscation to non-drug trafficking related money laundering and other offences.

As in all aspects of international organised crime, cooperation is vital if confiscation measures are to be successful against major criminals, who are skilled in concealing and putting their ill-gotten gains beyond the reach of the law through the full use of modern banking and communications technology and practice. The absolute need for international cooperation applies both to governments working together to ensure that judicial authorities can recover criminal proceeds and to authorities themselves to obtain and provide for each other information which will establish the movement of illicit proceeds and evidence against those involved. The established channels of cooperation are those described above in the context of mutual assistance.

European Convention on Extradition (Fiscal Offences) order 1993

Came in to force on 6 June 1994. This brought into effect the UK's ratification of the second Chapter of the Second Additional Protocol to the European Convention on Extradition. Chapter II of the Second Additional Protocol substituted a new Article 5 of the European Convention on Extradition which removed the restriction on extradition under that Convention for fiscal offences.

2.2
Confiscation

Jonathan Reuvid

The UN Convention and UK legislation against illicit drug trafficking

International cooperation against drug-trafficking and in facilitating the confiscation of its proceeds took a significant step forward in December 1988 with the adoption of the United Nations Convention against the Illicit Traffic in Narcotic Drugs and Psychotropic Substances. Specifically, parties to the Convention are required under Articles 3 and 5 to:

- establish criminal offences relating to money laundering;
- take legal powers to enable its authorities to trace, freeze and confiscate the proceeds of drug trafficking;
- co-operate in giving effect to restraint and confiscation orders made by the competent authorities of other parties.

Having ratified the Convention, the UK enacted legislation to meet the requirements not covered already under UK law with the Drug Trafficking Act 1994, The Criminal Justice (Scotland) Act 1987 and the Criminal Justice (Confiscation) (Northern Ireland) Order 1990. More recently, the Criminal Justice Act 1993, as noted on page 118, added the new offence of failing to report suspicions of money laundering as well as that of laundering the proceeds of non-drug trafficking crime.

Drug Trafficking Act 1994 and related Acts

The 1994 Act empowered the police and Customs and Excise to obtain information about suspected traffickers' financial affairs. If courts are satisfied that the information sought would be of value to a drug trafficking investigation, they can order disclosure of information, including records held by banks and other financial institutions. These powers may be used for the purpose of assisting in drug trafficking investigations abroad as well as in the UK.

Moreover, the assets of anyone suspected of drug trafficking may be restrained, even before proceedings are instituted against him, which prevents him from concealing his assets or transferring them abroad. Even if the funds are held by others on his behalf, they may be frozen by a restraint order applied for by the prosecution. The past practice, whereby suspects could conceal their funds before proceedings were brought against them so that they would be waiting for them once they had served their time in prison may now be thwarted. Once the decision has been taken to institute proceedings against suspects, their assets may be frozen.

When a person is convicted of a drug trafficking offence, the court must make a confiscation order depriving him of his proceeds, including those derived from trafficking for which he may not have been convicted and from payments or rewards received as a result of drug trafficking by others. The court assesses the full value of the proceeds of the offender's drug trafficking activities, including assets held in other countries, and issues a confiscation order equal to the sum assessed. For the purposes of assessment, the court is able to assume, in the absence of evidence to the contrary, that the proceeds of drug trafficking comprise the whole of the offender's property at the time of conviction, together with any property which has passed through his hands during the previous six years.

In this way the Act seeks to ensure that convicted drug traffickers suffer the confiscation of the full value of their illicit proceeds rather than those directly attributable to the offences for which they are convicted, thereby removing the incentive of vast profits.

Prior to the 1994 Act no legislation was available to prevent money laundering, whereby the proceeds of drug trafficking are passed through a series of financial institutions and centres in succession so as to make tracing difficult. The 1994 Act contains the further provision that anyone who knowingly holds, controls or invests another's profits derived from drug trafficking will have committed an offence, wherever in the world the trafficking occurred. Thus it is an offence to make drug assets appear to come from a legitimate source. In order to encourage disclosure, the 1994 Act provides statutory protection against actions for breach of contract to any person volunteering a suspicion that assets may be connected with drug trafficking.

As described in Part One, the money laundering of criminal proceeds which have entered the banking system is effected by transferring sums through a number of accounts in different banks in various financial centres. Laundered money is also invested in legitimate businesses and paid into 'shell' companies. Banks are required to be especially careful not to handle deposits known to have originated from drug trafficking. Of course, criminal proceeds can also be used to fund the purchase of goods for export or invested in stock exchange securities or real estate which can then be offered as collateral to raise loans in other countries. Under the 1994 Act, persons who assist in such arrangements are themselves liable for prosecution.

The Criminal Justice (International Co-operation Act) 1990, also referred to on page 117, strengthens the money laundering provisions of the 1994 Act by making it an offence for a person to launder his own proceeds or those of another person for the purpose of helping him to avoid prosecution for a drug trafficking offence or the making or enforcement of a confiscation order. The 1990 Act also provides for the authorisation of Customs or police officers to seize consignments of cash, on export or import, which they suspect of being connected to drug trafficking.

By extending the scope of the 1994 and 1990 Acts, as well as the Criminal Justice Act 1988 which itself enabled the courts to confiscate the proceeds of indictable offences, the Criminal Justice Act 1993 has brought within that law the full range of money laundering activities related to the 'proceeds of criminal conduct', defined as the benefit in relation to 'any person who has benefited from criminal conduct'. At the same time, the 1993 Act also defines 'insider dealing' as an indictable offence, a first attempt to bring within the control of the law some of the undisciplined excesses resulting from the City of London's 'big bang'.

The involvement of accessories and informants

Under Section 24 of the Drug Trafficking Act 1994, it is an offence for any person to assist another in disguising the true identity of drug trafficking proceeds. Specific activities which may constitute this offence are:

(a) enabling a drug trafficker to retain or control the proceeds of drug trafficking by concealment, removal from the jurisdiction, transfer to nominees or by any other means;
(b) placing funds derived from the proceeds of drug trafficking at the disposal of the drug trafficker; or
(c) acquiring property by way of investment of the proceeds of drug trafficking for the drug trafficker's benefit.

In order to encourage the disclosure of these laundering activities by third parties who may be involved, Section 24 provides that disclosure of a suspicion that money is derived from drug trafficking shall not constitute a breach of any obligations of confidentiality, thereby protecting the informant from the risk of civil action. Moreover, those who facilitate police investigations by going through the appearance of assisting in money laundering are protected from criminal prosecution.

The Criminal Justice (International Co-operation Act) 1990 widened the range of offences which may be committed by accessories to drug trafficking to include the laundering of the proceeds of drug trafficking of another person for the purposes of helping him to avoid prosecution for a drug trafficking offence or the making or enforcement of a confiscation order.

Of course, it is equally an offence for a person to launder his own proceeds of drug trafficking for the purpose of avoiding his own prosecution or the enforcement of a confiscation order against his own assets.

The 1990 Act also introduced a further activity which is designated an offence under the category of assisting another person to disguise the true identity of drug trafficking proceeds, that of acquiring property for no, or for inadequate, consideration, knowing or having reasonable grounds to suspect that it is the proceeds of drug trafficking.

The maximum penalty in the Crown Court for these additional offences is 14 years' imprisonment and/or a fine.

Finally, in the 1990 Act there are three new provisions relating to the assessment of realisable property and the mechanics of confiscation:

- Where it turns out that the value of the defendant's realisable property is greater than the court's original assessment, the amount recoverable under a confiscation order may be increased, provided that the amount of the realisable property has been assessed to be less than the value of the defendant's total proceeds from trafficking and the confiscation order has been made for the lesser amount. The revised amount of the confiscation order is limited to the value of proceeds assessed at the time the confiscation order was made.
- Interest may be added to confiscation orders which are not paid on time and is treated as part of the confiscation order. Any period of imprisonment in default may be increased accordingly.
- Under Part III of the Act, police and Customs and Excise officers are granted the power to detain, at import or export, cash which they suspect to be the proceeds of drug trafficking or intended for use in drug trafficking. With the authorisation of a magistrates' court, the cash may be detained for up to two years while investigations are carried out into its source. If a court is satisfied that the cash is connected to drug trafficking, the cash may be forfeited.

The Prevention of Terrorism (Temporary Provisions) Act 1989 contains provisions similar to those of the Drug Trafficking Act 1994 in respect of those assisting in the management and control of illegal funds. Section 11 creates an offence of assisting another to retain or control terrorist funds, whether by concealment, removal from the jurisdiction, transfer to nominees or otherwise. 'Terrorist funds' are defined to include monies used to further the commission of terrorist acts, the proceeds of the commission of terrorist acts and the resources of a proscribed terrorist organisation. Section 12 gives to those engaged in assisting in the disposition of terrorist funds protection similar to those engaged in laundering drug trafficking proceeds, so far as duties of confidentiality and participation in an investigation are concerned.

Section 13 and Schedule 4 of the 1989 Act also contain forfeiture provisions in respect of those convicted of fund raising on behalf of terrorist organisations, or the management of terrorist funds. The schedule empowers the courts to issue restraint orders in respect of property liable to forfeiture under the Act.

Part VI of the Criminal Justice Act 1988 introduced additional powers in regard to the confiscation and restraint of assets which relate to the generality of criminal offences where the offender has benefited by £10,000 or more. The essential differences between the 1988 Act and the Drug Trafficking Act 1994 are that under the former the courts are empowered to freeze assets in advance of the making of confiscation order, whereas under the latter the court may only confiscate the proceeds of the offences of which the defendant has been convicted and assumptions of guilt are not available.

The Criminal Justice Act 1993 clarifies and extends the provisions of the 1988 Act, and the operation of confiscation orders and their enactment, in respect of drug trafficking offences (Part II) and the proceeds of criminal conduct generally (Part III). Much of the 1993 Act takes the form of insertions into the provisions of the 1988 Act, covering the activities of assisting another to retain the benefit of criminal conduct and the disclosure of suspicions that any funds or investments are derived from or used in connection with criminal conduct.

In Section 29 Part III of the 1993 Act, any person's proceeds of criminal conduct are redefined to include 'any property which in whole or in part directly or indirectly represented in his hands his proceeds of criminal conduct'. Thus, through the evolution of successive legislation, provisions originally enacted to address the offences of those benefiting from the proceeds of drug trafficking and those assisting others in the money laundering and other disposition of their proceeds have been refined and their application extended to the general proceeds of criminal conduct and the confiscation of such proceeds.

The 1993 Act also amends the 1988 Act to include the offence of acquiring, using or having possession of property which he knows to represent, in whole or in part directly or indirectly, another person's proceeds of criminal conduct. It is a defence to a charge of committing this offence that the person charged acquired or used the property or had possession of it for adequate consideration. However, the consideration is defined as inadequate if:

(a) the value of the consideration paid by the person acquiring the property is significantly less than the value of the property;
(b) the value of the consideration paid by the person using or having possession of the property is significantly less than the value of his use or possession of the property.

Moreover, the provision for any person of services or goods which are of assistance to him in criminal conduct shall not be treated as 'adequate consideration'.

Protection against prosecution and against breach of confidentiality is provided under the 1993 Act to anyone who discloses to a constable a suspicion or a belief before, and in some cases after, the event that any property represents, in whole or in part directly or indirectly, another person's proceeds of criminal conduct.

The 1993 Act establishes, as in the case of the proceeds of drug trafficking in previous Acts, that it is an offence for anyone to conceal or disguise any property which represents his proceeds of criminal conduct, or who converts or transfers that property or removes it from the jurisdiction, in order to avoid prosecution or the making or enforcement in his case of a confiscation order. A parallel offence is committed if anyone, knowing or having reasonable grounds to suspect that any property represents another person's criminal proceeds, performs the same actions for the purpose of assisting another person to avoid prosecution of an offence or the making or enforcement of a confiscation order against him.

In addition, the 1993 Act establishes the offence of 'tipping off' in relation to money laundering and the acquisition, use and possession of the proceeds of criminal conduct. A person is guilty of this offence if:

(a) he knows or suspects that a constable is acting, or is planning to act in connection with an investigation which is being, or is about to be, conducted; and
(b) discloses to any other person information or any other matter which is likely to prejudice that investigation or proposed investigation.

Equally, a person is guilty of the same offence if he knows or suspects that a disclosure has been made to a constable and discloses to another person information or any other matter which is likely to prejudice any investigation which might be made following the disclosure.

These provisions do not apply to disclosure by a professional legal adviser to a client, or his representative, in connection with the giving of legal advice or to any person in contemplation of, or in connection with, legal proceedings and for the purpose of such proceedings, provided that any information or other matter is not disclosed with a view to furthering any criminal purpose.

The penalties for summary conviction on the offence of 'tipping off' are imprisonment for up to six months or a fine or both; for conviction on indictment the maximum term of imprisonment is increased to five years.

Part III of the 1993 Act also contains provisions for the application of sections of the Criminal Justice Act 1988 to Scotland and the enforcement of Northern Ireland orders in respect of the proceeds of criminal conduct. It also clarifies and extends provisions for the prosecution of money laundering and other offences by order of the Commissioners of Customs and Excise.

Part IV of the 1993 Act deals with confiscation orders, revised assessments and enforcement relating to the financing of terrorism and offences related to the proceeds of terrorist-related activities, thereby amending the Northern Ireland (Emergency

Provisions Act) 1991 and the Prevention of Terrorism (Temporary Provisions) Act 1989, which are outside the scope of this book.

Finally, Part V of the Criminal Justice Act 1993 addresses the offence of insider dealing and replaces in full the Company Securities (Insider Dealing) Act 1985. The provisions of Part V are examined separately in section 2.4.

The Acts and Conventions in practice

The effectiveness of the Acts described is dependant upon the levels of success in detection and investigation for which, in the UK, the NCIS bears the principal responsibility. Within the NCIS there is a Financial Intelligence Unit manned jointly by police and Customs officers. The unit receives financial intelligence, mainly from banks and other financial institutions on a national basis, about funds where it is suspected that they are derived from drug trafficking or the money laundering process.

In UK terms, since the Criminal Justice (International Co-operation) Act 1990 came into force, the number and quality of disclosures of suspected drug proceeds made by institutions to the Financial Intelligence Unit has increased steadily as knowledge of the Act has spread and financial institutions have gained confidence in the confidentiality of the disclosure arrangements. The sums of money and value of assets frozen and consequently confiscated have likewise grown steadily.

The formation of the Financial Action Task Force on Money Laundering (FATF), established by the G7 Group of industrialised countries in 1989 was a milestone in the development of coordinated international anti-money laundering policies. It followed directly from the 1988 Vienna Convention which prompted many countries to adopt either a partial or a complete set of criminal and regulatory policies against the laundering of the proceeds of crime.

In February 1990, drawing on the authority of the Vienna Convention and the proceedings of the Basel Committee on Banking Regulations and Supervisory Practices of the same year, FATF published a report containing 40 recommendations for combatting money-laundering. All 40 recommendations have been enacted subsequently by members of the Council of Europe Convention on the Laundering of the Proceeds of Crime of 1991 which set out to harmonize the anti-money laundering policies of the 12 European countries. As Saul Froomkin notes in his introduction to this book, the first member of the Council to ratify the convention was the UK in September 1992, followed by:

Australia	
Austria	Ireland
Belgium	Italy
Bulgaria	Luxembourg
Cyprus	Netherlands
Denmark	Portugal
France	Spain
Germany	Sweden
Greece	Switzerland

Other non-member states of the European Council invited to sign the Convention include the United States and Canada.

The demand for financial intelligence, using the state of art techniques of IT and data communications has produced new and specialised agencies, the international counterparts of the NCIS Financial Intelligence Unit, such as FINCEN in the USA, TRACFIN in France and AUSTRAC in Australia. FATF membership now consists of representatives of not only the EU and OECD countries, but also Singapore, Hong Kong and the Gulf Co-operation Council. Inevitably, organised crime is reacting to the development of more effective anti-money laundering strategies and coordinated investigation techniques, by employing more professional advisers as well as more complex and sophisticated schemes.

The EC money laundering directive

In June 1991, the EEC (now EU) Council of Economic and Finance Ministers adopted a Directive (91/308/EEC) on the prevention of the use of the financial system for money laundering purposes. Member States were required to implement the Directive by 1 January 1993.

The Directive demands the prohibition of the laundering of money derived from the proceeds of drug trafficking and permits Member States to widen the scope of 'money laundering', as defined in Article 1, to include the proceeds of any other criminal activity.

Among the key provisions of the Directive are:

Article 3 which states that Member States shall ensure that credit and financial institutions require identification of their customers by means of supporting evidence when they enter into business relations;

Article 6 which places a duty on Member States to ensure that credit and financial institutions cooperate fully with the authorities responsible for combatting money laundering;

Article 8 which requires a prohibition against disclosure ('tipping off') to a customer or third party that information has been passed on to the authorities or that a money laundering investigation is being undertaken.

Bilateral confiscation agreements

The selection of countries who wish to conclude among themselves bilateral agreements to trace, freeze, and confiscate the proceeds of drug trafficking, money laundering and other crimes is dependent upon several factors. The countries which it is most desirable to include are those which encompass major financial centres or are drug producers or transit countries. However, in order to be eligible, such countries must have legislation which is compatible with that of the countries with whom they form treaties.

Nevertheless, bilateral and multilateral agreements have proliferated in the last few years, including the US and Russia pact on policing of July 1994, cited by Saul Froomkin. The UK alone has concluded bilateral confiscation agreements or arrangements with 34 countries and territories:

Anguilla	Colombia	Nigeria
Argentina	Ecuador	Panama
Australia	Gibraltar	Paraguay
Bahamas	Grenada	Saudi Arabia
Bahrain	Guyana	South Africa
Barbados	Hong Kong	Spain
Bermuda	India	Sweden
Bolivia	Malaysia	Switzerland
British Virgin Isl's.	Mexico	Thailand
Canada	Montserrat	USA
Cayman Islands	Netherlands	Uruguay

Some of these arrangements are restricted to cooperation in respect of the proceeds of drug trafficking; however, others apply more generally to the proceeds of any criminal activity.

Under most of these agreements and arrangements the confiscation orders of the other States which are parties to these agreements can be enforced under UK legislation through the UK courts. In addition, the restraint powers referred to in previous sections can be invoked to prevent dealings in the property of a drug trafficker in the United Kingdom, where proceedings have been or are to be instituted in a designated State. In this way, the British High Court can prevent dealings in the assets of a drug trafficker while court proceedings are still in progress in the designated State, and can direct that property be realised to enforce a confiscation order made by a foreign court.

Returning to the narrower field of drug traffic, there are also 111 States including the United Kingdom and other members of the EU, as well as the EU itself, which had ratified the 1988 Convention against Illicit Traffic in Narcotic Drugs and Psychotropic Substances as at 9 May 1995. A full list of those countries, in the date order of their ratification is given in Appendix II.

In 1991, the Seized Asset Fund was set up in the United Kingdom with the objective of recycling monies obtained through the enforcement of international agreements to assist in the fight against drugs. In the year 1992-3 the fund totalled £3.2 million, derived mainly from money gifted to the Metropolitan Police and HM Customs by the USA in 1990 and 1991. Of this total, approximately £1 million was placed in a separate, dedicated fund to help meet the additional costs to the police of international drug investigations; the balance of some £2.2 million was distributed to 147 projects and schemes.

Projects which have been supported from the Seized Assets Fund include treatment services for drug misusers, overseas assistance and prevention education and 'state of the art' enforcement equipment for the police and Customs.

2.3
Tracing the Proceeds of Fleeing Money

John Forbes

The nature of fraud

Fraud can be analysed into three components: the initial theft, the concealment of that theft, and the conversion of the stolen assets into usable funds. Looking at these in turn, the management of an organisation will put in place internal controls to minimise the risk of theft. However, no system of controls is absolutely foolproof against a determined insider. Also, most systems rely on the segregation of duties between (for example) those responsible for initiating transactions, and those who authorise or approve their financial value. Thus collusion between different people can neutralise such controls.

Theft is certainly *possible* in practically all business situations. The secondary aim of the organisation's internal control system is, therefore, to detect any actual thefts as soon as possible after the event. Here the fraudster will attempt to maximise the delay between the theft and its detection by concealing the theft.

It is this element of concealment which distinguishes fraud from 'simple' robbery. The concealment, and hence the delay in detection of the theft, gives the fraudster time. First, he needs time to distance himself from the site of the theft, especially if he is an internal member of the organisation. Second, the more time he has available for the conversion of the stolen assets, the more effectively he will be able to convert them into usable funds.

Conversion and laundering

The conversion process depends on the nature of the stolen assets. Broadly, the fraudster will have stolen either assets (goods or information) which he has to sell, or money in the form of cash or a bank credit. Let's consider the first category; the fraudster will either attempt to pass off the assets as legitimately his, or will use criminal acquaintances to 'fence' the goods. In both cases the defrauded organisation can use intelligence-gathering to attempt to recover its goods (or intercept its information). For instance, there is a well established international intelligence network relating to stolen works of art and antiques; in the UK the art trade and insurance companies have set up the Art Loss Register database, through which £14 million worth of stolen art and antiques have been recovered in the past four years. Alternatively, through co-operation with its national police, (and internationally through their links with Interpol) the organisation can look for intelligence from the criminal community.

Suppose, however, that the fraudster has managed to sell the stolen goods. He is now in the same position as the fraudster who has stolen money; unless the amounts involved are small he will need to launder the funds. This is for two reasons: cloaking the funds with legitimacy means they can then be used for any purpose: and it also frustrates attempts at recovery by the defrauded organisation.

The laundering of the funds can take many forms, but will usually involve a series of transactions transferring the funds from one point to the next. These transfers may have the following features:

- they will happen quickly;
- they may use more than one jurisdiction;
- in particular, the jurisdictions used may include those which are 'opaque' (not easily accessible) to outside investigators – jurisdictions which are considered tax havens usually fall into this category;
- the funds may change their nature – for instance, rather than a simple transfer from one bank account to another, the identity of the funds may be disguised by multiple transfers –

'layering and integrating';
- the named owners of bank accounts in a chain of transactions will often themselves be foreign (to the jurisdiction of the bank account) companies or trusts, which renders these account holders opaque to the investigator.

Figure 2.3.1 below illustrates an actual trail of bank account transfers.

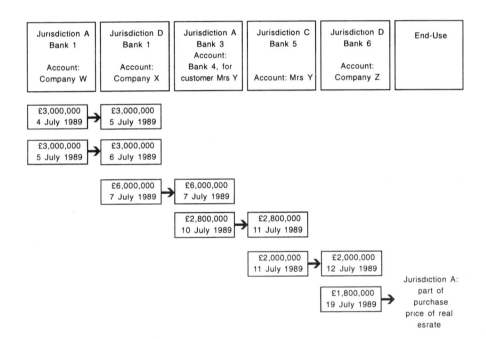

Figure 2.3.1 *A trail of bank account transfers*

The start of the trail

The investigator seeking to trace the proceeds of fleeing money needs to know the starting point of the trail, the point where the money or asset disappeared from the organisation. In the above example, the initial theft from Company 'W' occurred as the two payments of £3,000,000 shown. His investigations will, therefore, be aimed at reconstructing the details of that trail thereafter.

In this example the path of the initial theft is clear, involving only two fraudulent transfers out of the organisation. Often, however, an organisation may discover a 'hole' in its assets without any clear indication of where they have gone, or how much is missing. There may have been large scale theft over a long period of time, by more than one person; the assets stolen may never have been properly recorded or (especially in the case of theft of information) their value may not be clear.

In these cases the investigator will have to establish the extent and method of the thefts. It goes beyond the scope of this article to discuss this in detail, although a knowledge of information technology will almost certainly be necessary, if any of the defrauded organisation's relevant records are held on computer. Specialist interrogation software can be used to detect significant or unusual transactions or trends.

Managing the investigative team

Having determined the starting point, the asset tracing investigation is based on obtaining and analysing information to illustrate the subsequent trail. This requires the proper mix of investigative skills; an investigation will probably, over its life, involve:

- commercial lawyers;
- investigative ('forensic') accountants;
- information technology specialists;
- the police.

And that is a minimum list. Specific industry experts may be required; insurance companies may wish to participate. In particular, if the fraud involves different jurisdictions there will almost certainly be a need for legal advice in each jurisdiction.

Efficient liaison with police is very important. Police usually have powers available to them beyond those available to the defrauded organisation under civil law. If the police can be persuaded that there has been an act of criminal fraud, their investigations can be much quicker and wider-ranging than those of the organisation alone. In particular, the police may be able to act effectively in obtaining information from other countries, depending on the jurisdictions involved. Often funds may have been transferred into a jurisdiction where there is no mechanism under civil law whereby the defrauded organisation can obtain information such as bank records – liaison with the police may be the *only* means of getting the information.

Managing the information

The information obtained will be diverse, for instance internal records of the defrauded organisation; interviews of people involved; Company and Land Registry records; bank records; press reports. The process is iterative; once one transaction in the trail has been worked out the investigator will attempt to follow the funds through the next. This will often require a new Court application for disclosure of new information, where the Court will require some proof that the funds have gone to (for example) the bank concerned. Having obtained disclosure of the details of that next step, the investigator will proceed to the subsequent one, and so on.

Efficient management of the information obtained is critical to the success of the investigation. Not wasting time on the irrelevant is as important as not overlooking any useful detail. Also, information may appear unimportant when first discovered, only for its actual importance to be revealed later. To this end investigators should consider the use of computerised document management systems in all but the simplest investigations. These systems are databases into which data from all documents discovered during the investigation (or even optically-scanned images of the entire documents) can be entered. Subsequently, the database can be interrogated to search for connections between names or dates. For instance, in Figure 2.3.1, the investigator may take several months to discover the step in the trail where the funds are transferred to Company 'Z'. He can, however, then go back and search for all references to Company 'Z' in the database.

Recovery of the stolen funds

The investigator's aim is, of course, recovery of the stolen funds. Using the example of Figure 2.3.1, the real estate would be claimed. In addition, the investigator would attempt to obtain Court orders freezing any funds remaining in banks 3, 5 and 6 so as to try to capture the balance of the £6 million. In reality, however, some or all of the funds may have already been dissipated. The second path of recovery is, therefore, to look to seize the fraudster's other assets. This may be fruitful if the fraudster is wealthy, but often his identifiable assets (house, car, other bank accounts) will be less than the costs of the action to seize them.

The third path of recovery is to look for other individuals or organisations who have assisted in the fraud. It may be possible to prove a criminal conspiracy, and so to attack the assets of the co-fraudsters. However, even if this is not possible, it may be possible to use other legal means against third parties. For example, the investigator will look for negligence or breach of trust by advisers to, or auditors of, the defrauded organisation, or by bankers or others involved in the trail of funds. Suppose that the initial theft occurred as the result of a forged cheque; the investigator will consider whether the organisation's bank should have exercised more care in scrutinising the forgery.

Conclusion

In summary, some of the major factors in successfully tracing the proceeds of fleeing money are:

- speed of action;
- intelligence at the conversion stage;
- assembling and co-ordinating a multi-disciplinary team;
- considering all areas of attack against the fraudster, his possible accomplices, and third parties;
- efficient use of information technology.

Do all of this and you have a *chance* of recovering the stolen assets. The final factor you need is common sense; a puzzle created by one mind can be solved by another, so just ask yourself what would I have done if I were the fraudster?"

2.4
Insider Dealing

Jonathan Reuvid

The relatively new offence of 'insider dealing', first addressed specifically in The Company Securities (Insider Dealing) Act 1985 and referred to in The Financial Services Act 1986, is redefined and legislated against more effectively in the Criminal Justice Act 1993 which replaces in full the 1985 Act and the relevant sections of the 1986 Act. Insider dealing is categorised as the companion offence of fraud and corruption.

Fraud and corruption

Offences of fraud are defined in the Criminal Law Act 1977 and in the Theft Acts of 1968 and 1978. The Criminal Justice Act 1987 established the Serious Fraud Office (SFO) which is responsible for investigating serious and complex fraud cases in England and Wales (usually those involving the loss of £5 million or more).

Likewise in Scotland, where fraud is punishable under common law, the Criminal Justice (Scotland) Act 1987 conferred identical powers to those of the SFO on officers nominated by the Lord Advocate.

There are three main statutes which apply to corrupt activities, referred to collectively as the Prevention of Corruption Acts 1889 to 1916. The first of these anti-corruption Acts is the Public Bodies Corrupt Practices Act 1889, which made it an offence for someone 'corruptly to solicit, receive or agree to receive, for himself or any other person, any gift, fee, loan, reward, or any other advantage as an inducement to or reward for any member, officer or servant of a public body doing or not doing anything in relation to any matter in which the public body is concerned'. Similarly, it is an offence corruptly to give, promise to offer such a gift, loan, fee, reward or any other advantage. Conviction of an offence under this Act for a second time, renders the convicted person also liable to disqualification from public office for life and loss of voting rights for five years.

Originally, a 'public body' in this Act was defined as a local authority, or any other body which has powers in relation to local government, public health or poor law. The scope of the law was extended to other public bodies, including central government, and to businesses by the Prevention of Corruption Act 1906. Subsequently, in the Prevention of Corruption Act 1916 the scope of the 1889 Act was extended further to encompass 'local and public authorities of all descriptions'. This latter Act also provides that in a prosecution for corruption, if it is proved that a gift has been given to a Crown servant or employee or a public body by or on behalf of a person holding or seeking to obtain a contract with the Crown or public body, the gift shall be deemed to have been given and received corruptly unless the defendant can prove the contrary.

Under the influence of the media, the focus of public opprobrium in the UK seems to have moved away from corruption towards standards of personal behaviour and the peccadilloes of people in public office or the public eye. Perhaps it is a sign of the times that in mid-nineties Britain that self-confessed cases of Members of Parliament accepting fees for the placing of questions in Parliament, which would appear to be prima facie offences under the Prevention of Corrupt Acts, have been castigated by the newspapers as examples of ubiquitous 'sleaze' rather than designated as alleged cases of corruption.

Part V of the Criminal Justice Act 1993

Part V of the Act defines the offence of insider dealing in the following specific terms:

An individual who has information as an insider is guilty of insider dealing if ... he deals in securities that are price-affected in relation to the information' in the following circumstances: namely, 'that the acquisition or disposal in question occurs on a regulated market, or that the person dealing relies on a professional intermediary or is himself acting as a professional intermediary.

An individual who has information as an insider is also guilty of insider dealing if 'he discloses the information, otherwise than in the proper performance of the functions of his employment, office or profession to another person' or alternatively if he encourages someone else to deal in securities that are price-affected (whether or not that other person knows it) in relation to the information, knowing or having reasonable cause to believe that the dealing would take place in the circumstances specified above.

There are, however, a series of defences which are effective against charges of insider dealing if the accused person, having dealt in the securities in question, is able to show:

(a) that he did not expect at the time that dealing would result in a profit attributable to the information in question being price-sensitive in relation to the securities;
(b) that at the time he believed, on reasonable grounds, that the information had been disclosed sufficiently widely for none of those taking part in dealing to be prejudiced by not having the information;
(c) that he would have done what he did, even if he had not had the information.

Similar defences are available to individuals accused of insider dealing by virtue of encouraging another person to deal in securities or by virtue of disclosure of information.

The securities to which Part V applies are listed in Schedule 2 to the Act, which identifies the following:

- shares, being shares and stock in the capital of a company;
- debt securities, comprising any instrument creating or acknowledging indebtedness, including debentures, debenture stock, loan stock, bonds, and certificates of deposit;

- warrants, being any right to subscribe for shares or debt securities;
- depositary receipts, being the rights thereunder;
- options to acquire or dispose of any of the securities defined within the schedule;
- futures, being rights under a contract for the acquisition or disposal of relevant securities under which delivery is to be made at a future date and at a price agreed when the contract is made;
- contracts for differences, defined as rights under a contract which does not provide for the delivery of securities, but whose purpose, or pretended purpose, is to secure a profit or avoid a loss by reference to fluctuations in:

(a) a share index or similar factor connected with any of the securities listed in the schedule;
(b) the price of any of the securities listed in the schedule;
(c) the interest rate offered on money placed on deposit.

The Act allows for amendments by Parliamentary order to the Schedule at the instigation of the Treasury.

In further sections of Part V 'inside information' is defined more closely as information which:

(a) relates to particular securities or to a particular issuer or issuers of securities and not to securities in general or to issuers of securities generally;
(b) is specific or precise;
(c) has not been made public; and
(d) if it were made public would be likely to have a significant effect on the price of any securities.

and a person having information as an 'insider', if and only if:

(a) it, and he knows that it is, inside information; and
(b) he has it, and knows that he has it, from an inside source. A person has information from an inside source, if and only if he has it through being a director, employee or shareholder or an issuer of securities or has access to the information by virtue of his employment, office or profession. Alternatively, the direct

or indirect source of his information may be a person in a similar position or circumstances.

In the interests of clarity, Part V of the Act also defines closely the phrase 'made public', in relation to information, the terms 'professional intermediary', and 'regulated market' and 'issuer'.

The penalties for an individual found guilty of insider dealing on summary judgment are imprisonment for a period of not more than six months or a fine not exceeding the statutory maximum. On conviction on indictment, the penalties are a fine or imprisonment for not more than seven years or both.

2.5
Extradition

Jonathan Reuvid

Origins

The original Multilateral European Convention on Extradition was opened for signature by member states of the Council of Europe Council in September 1957; the final text was adopted at a meeting of the Council on 13 December 1957 and entered into force on 18 April 1960. The Convention had its origins in Recommendation 51 (16), adopted on 8 December 1951 in the 37th Session of the Consultative Assembly of the Council of Europe, 'on the preparatory measures to be taken to achieve the conclusion of a European Convention on Extradition'.

Subsequently, the Committee of Ministers instructed the Secretary General to convene a Committee of Government Experts to examine the recommendation and to study the question as to whether mutually acceptable extradition principles should be implemented by the establishment of a multilateral convention or should simply serve as a basis for bilateral conventions. The preliminary draft multilateral convention was the outcome of a series of sessions of the Committee of Experts held in Strasbourg between October 1953 and February 1956 which included consultation in September 1955 with a competent sub-committee of the Assembly Committee on Legal and Administrative Questions.

In June 1969, the Council of Europe organised a meeting for the persons responsible at national level for the application of the Convention. The participants in that meeting discussed the various problems arising in connection with the application of the Convention and made a number of proposals for improving its operation. These conclusions were examined by the ECCP at its 20th Plenary Session in 1971 which set up a sub-committee (no XXX1) to examine the problems raised and to propose the appropriate means for implementing the conclusions reached at the 1969 meeting.

Sub-committee XXX1 first elaborated the Additional Protocol which was opened for signature on 15 October 1975 and then examined a number of other questions relating to the practical application of the Convention. In the course of successive meetings through to March 1976, the Second Additional Protocol was prepared. At its 25th Plenary Session in 1976, the ECCP decided to enlarge the composition of sub-committee XXX1 to examine the draft text, including experts from all member states as well as from the contracting parties which were not members of the Council of Europe. The enlarged sub-committee met in September 1976 and March 1977 and an amended draft Additional Protocol was submitted to the 26th Plenary Session of the ECCP in May 1977 which decided to transmit it to the Committee of Ministers for approval.

The Second Additional Protocol [1]

The Second Additional Protocol to the European Convention on Extradition was drawn up within the Council of Europe by a committee of governmental experts under the authority of the European Committee on Crime Problems (ECCP) and was adopted at the 279th meeting of Ministers' Deputies in November 1977. The Protocol became open to member states for signature on 17 March 1978.

The topics covered by the Second Additional Protocol to the European Convention on Extradition in its articles, pertinent to the treatment of offences relating to international economic crime, are the following:

---

1.   The UK reserved the right not to accept Chapters I, III or V of the Second Additional Protocol.

- extension of accessory extradition to offences carrying only a pecuniary sanction (Chapter I);
- extension of the Convention to fiscal offences (Chapter II);
- judgments in absentia (Chapter III);
- amnesty (Chapter IV);
- communication of requests for extradition (Chapter V).

The most significant points addressed in each chapter are summarised in the order in which they appear.

Chapter I – Accessory Extradition

In some states the Law draws a distinction between criminal offences (those punishable by criminal penalties) with other offences dealt with by pecuniary sanctions, which are not regarded as criminal penalties. For example, in Germany (FDR) there are offences against public order (Ordnungswidrigkeiten), which are dealt with by the administrative authorities, but are subject to appeal to the ordinary criminal courts.

Under the Convention, as adopted originally, minor criminal offences which carry only a fine, as well as the other types of offence described above, could not give rise to extradition under Article 2.2, because they did not fulfil the specified conditions regarding the nature of the sanction.

However, such offences may cause significant social harm; thus, Chapter I extends the scope of the application of accessory extradition permissible under Article 2.2 to include these offences. Therefore, it is possible for the requesting State to obtain extradition also for an offence which is subject to a criminal fine or any other pecuniary sanction.

In the original Convention the principle of double criminality is established in the definition of extraditable offences in Article 2.1 which states that extradition shall be granted in respect of offences which are punishable by imprisonment or detention under the laws of both the requesting and the requested Party. However, the Additional Protocol establishes that it is not necessary for the offences to be punishable by the same kind of sanction in both States. The Protocol follows the principle laid down, for instance, in Article II.2 of the bilateral Swiss-German

Agreement of 13 November 1969 which supplements the
European Convention on Extradition.

Article 12 of the Convention specifies that the documents to
be submitted in support of a request for accessory extradition
are to include the original or an authenticated copy of the conviction and sentence or detention order or of the warrant of arrest.
The Protocol relaxes this requirement to include, instead of a
warrant of arrest, any other document showing that a charge
has been brought against the person concerned.

Chapter II – Fiscal Offences

The Second Additional Protocol strengthens Article 5 of the
Convention by insisting that extradition shall take place irrespective of any arrangements between the contracting parties
whenever the fiscal offence, under the law of the requesting
State, corresponds, under the law of the requested State, to an
offence of the same nature. Article 5 had provided that extradition for such offences would be granted only if the contracting
parties had previously decided so in respect of any such offence
or category of offences.

For a long time, it had been considered that fiscal offences
should not be treated as ordinary offences on the grounds that
they were similar to military or political offences which had not
given rise traditionally to extradition. It was held that it was not
incumbent upon one State to protect the finances of another, and
therefore States shrank from granting extradition when the victim
was another State, rather than a private person.

More recently, there have been changes in the approach to
criminal policy and the need for closer international cooperation
in this field is now recognised. In view of the damage to society
caused by economic offences, it is now accepted that there is no
justification for differentiating in matters of extradition between
fiscal and 'ordinary' offences which are placed on the same
footing by Chapter II of the Protocol.

Since the laws of member States differ in respect of the
constituent elements of the various offences connected with taxes,
duties, customs and exchange, difficulties in interpretation have
been addressed by adopting the words 'taxes, duties, customs and

exchange' in Chapter II of the Protocol (as in Article 5 of the Convention) rather than the less definitive term 'fiscal offence'.

Moreover, paragraph 1 of Chapter II provides that extradition shall take place 'if the offence, under the law of the requested Party, corresponds to an offence of the same nature'. Thus, extradition is to be granted not only where an act is punishable as the same fiscal offence in the requesting and requested States, but also where an act of the same nature as that underlying the request for extradition would be punishable in the requested State. One example of such an underlying act is the evasion of tax or duty by giving untrue information in a document used as a basis for deciding the amount of that tax or duty payable.

The consequence of an absence of definition for the term 'fiscal offence' is that the requested State has wide discretion in evaluating the eventual nature of the offence. Paragraph 2 of Article II of the Protocol states specifically that extradition may not be refused on the grounds that the requested Party does not impose the same kind of tax or duty as the law of the requesting Party, reinforcing the theme that the essential constituent elements of the offence shall be decisive.

Extradition in respect of fiscal offences is granted 'in accordance with the provisions of the Convention', including the conditions concerning the level of penalties for the offence in question specified, inter alia, in Article 2 of the Convention.

Chapter III – Judgments in Absentia

'Judgments in absentia', properly so-called, are defined in Article 21.2 of the European Convention on the International Validity of Criminal Judgments as judgments rendered after a hearing at which the sentenced person was not personally present. (They do not include *ordonnances penales*.)

The drafting sub-committee of the Protocol decided that the text should not be based on Articles 21 et seq. of the European Convention on the International Validity of Criminal Judgments, for the reason that it was inappropriate to transfer the machinery of that Convention to a different context. Instead, paragraph 1 of Chapter III of the Protocol, which provides for a procedure proper to the Extradition Convention, allows the requested Party to refuse extradition if the proceedings leading to the judgment did not satisfy the rights of defence recognised as being due to everyone charged with a criminal offence. An exception to the principle is made if the requesting Party gives an assurance, considered sufficient, to guarantee to the person concerned the right to a retrial which safeguards his rights of defence, and that such a remedy would be effective. In such a case, extradition shall be granted.

In effect, Chapter III of the Protocol recognises that exemption from the obligation to extradite should apply if there has been a violation of any of the generally acknowledged rights of defence, in particular those specified in the whole of Article 6.3 of the Human Rights Convention to which the Netherlands had drawn attention in its reservation to the Extradition Convention.

The minimum rules aimed at guaranteeing the accused's rights as laid down in the European Convention for the Protection of Human Rights and Fundamental Freedoms, specified under resolution (75) 11 of the Committee of Ministers of the Council of Europe of 21 May 1975, may serve for the purpose of determining the scope of the phrase 'rights of defence' used in Chapter III of the Protocol.

Having been extradited upon receipt of sufficient assurances by the requested Party, the surrendered person concerned may accept the judgment rendered against him in his absence or demand a retrial, as provided in the last paragraph of Chapter III of the Protocol. If the domestic law of the requesting Party does not allow a retrial, assurances will be insufficient and there is no obligation for the requested Party to extradite.

A further means of strengthening the legal interests of the person to be extradited is provided by paragraph 2 of Chapter III which states that communication of the judgment rendered in absentia is not to be regarded by the requesting State as a formal notification. The main purpose of this provision is to ensure that the person who is the subject of the extradition proceedings does not find himself with only a very short time in which to register his opposition, whereas the formalities relating to his handing over may take several weeks or even months.

Chapter IV – Amnesty

The original Extradition Convention was silent on the question whether an amnesty granted in a requested State is a ground for refusing extradition. Chapter IV of the Protocol provides a solution based on examples contained in prior bilateral extradition agreements, but does not address amnesties in the requesting Party, because the drafting sub-committee considered it unlikely that a State would apply for an extradition for an offence in respect of which it had previously granted an amnesty itself.

Chapter IV provides that an amnesty (relating either to criminal prosecution or to the enforcement of sentences) in the requested State is a barrier to extradition from that State only if it has jurisdiction over the offence concurrently with the requesting State.

Chapter V – Communication of Requests for Extradition

Article 12.1 of the Convention, as adopted originally, provides for extradition requests to be communicated through the diplomatic channels. Chapter V seeks to provide a more expeditious method of communication, having regard to the delays experienced in some States through the use of diplomatic channels and possible difficulties in submitting a request for extradition within the maximum period of eighteen days provided for in Article 16 of the Convention where a request for provisional arrest had been made.

Therefore, Chapter V replaces paragraph 1 of Article 12 of the Convention with the following provisions:

> The request shall be made in writing and shall be addressed by the Ministry of Justice of the requesting Party to the Ministry of Justice of the requested Party; however, use of the diplomatic channel is not excluded. Other means of communication may be arranged by direct agreement between two or more Parties.

In those States, such as England and Wales, where there is no Ministry of Justice, the term is understood to mean the department of government, by whatever name it is known (eg the Home

Office), which is responsible for the administration of criminal justice.

Chapter VI – Final Clauses of the Protocol

In Chapter VI procedures for signature, ratification, acceptance or approval are detailed. Under Article 6, Member States of the Council of Europe which have signed but not ratified the Extradition Convention may sign the Protocol before ratifying the Convention, but the Protocol may be ratified, accepted or approved only by member States which have ratified the Convention. Conversely, there is no obligation on a member State ratifying the Convention in the future to become a contracting party to the Protocol. Likewise, the Protocol may be acceded to by a non-member State only if it has acceded to the Extradition Convention.

Accession to the Convention by non-member States of the Council of Europe is conditional upon invitation from the Committee of Ministers, but no such invitation is required for accession to the Protocol so that a non-member State which has at any time acceded to the Convention has an automatic right (but no obligation) to accede to the Protocol.

Article 9.1 lays down the general principle that, in the absence of a declaration to the contrary, existing reservations to the Extradition Convention also apply to the Protocol. There is also provision for any reservations to be withdrawn.

Article 9.2 provides for contracting Parties not to accept one or more of the four chapters of the Protocol and to limit their non-acceptance of Chapter II (Fiscal Offences) to certain offences or categories of offence. They may also limit their non-acceptance of Chapter III (Judgments in Absentia) to paragraph 2. These particular provisions were included in order to encourage States which, for the time being, find it impossible to accept all chapters to become, nevertheless, Parties to the Protocol.

UK domestic legislation

The Extradition Act 1989 came into force in September 1989. It consolidated changes to extradition arrangements made in the Criminal Justice Act 1988 (which enabled the UK to ratify the European Convention on Extradition), the Fugitive Offenders Act 1967 and the Extradition Act 1870, the latter being maintained in existence as Schedule 1 to the 1989 Act, as well as amendments to give effect to recommendations of the Law Commission and the Scottish Law Commission. It provides that an offence is an extradition offence if it attracts on indictment a sentence of 12 months or more in both countries. It also contains a number of common features internationally recognised as basic principles in extradition arrangements. For countries other than those which have ratified the European Convention on Extradition, a person's return also depends on whether a prima facie case can be shown against him.

The Extradition Act 1989 is the legislation which governs the UK extradition arrangements. Within the Commonwealth, extradition is possible if countries have enacted reciprocal national legislation reflecting an agreed Commonwealth extradition scheme. In the case of foreign states (defined in the Act), it is read in conjunction with any multilateral treaty such as the European Convention on Extradition or bilateral treaty, eg US/UK Treaty.

As far as extradition to and from the Irish Republic is concerned, although the UK and the Republic of Ireland are both parties to the European Convention on Extradition, it has been agreed that extradition arrangements between the two countries will continue to operate under the backing of Warrants (Republic of Ireland) Act 1965 and the reciprocal Irish legislation. This is more simple and straightforward method of returning people to and from the Republic of Ireland. All crimes punishable by six (as opposed to 12, for the rest of Europe) months' imprisonment are extraditable.

Part Three
PREVENTION

3.1
The Focus on Money Laundering

Jonathan Reuvid

The Vienna Convention of 1988 was a watershed in the development of coordinated international regulatory and policing action designed both to treat and prevent money laundering. Until then, only the United States and a few other countries had adopted specific domestic anti-laundering policies. As noted in Chapter 2.2, the Financial Action Task Force on Money Laundering (FATF) was established by the G7 Group of industrialised countries in the year following, and its 40 recommendations for combatting money-laundering were embodied in the Council of Europe Convention on the Laundering of the Proceeds of Crime in 1991. Effectively, the Convention harmonized the anti-money laundering policies of the EU member States, with certain other States, notably the United States, Canada and Australia joining as signatories.

In 1992 the Organization of American States promulgated its own recommended set of measures, based on the FATF recommendations, for Latin American States. By 1994 an international anti-money laundering system of soft laws was in place, providing a coordinated set of domestic, regional or international mechanisms. The system responds to the common strategic priorities of:

- fighting organised crime by recovering the proceeds of criminal activity;
- protecting the transparency of financial and economic systems from infiltration by organised criminal groups.

In his paper to the Twelfth International Symposium on Economic Crime at Jesus College, Cambridge in September 1994, Ernesto Savona, professor of Criminology, School of Law, University of Trento, Italy, noted that:

> these policies require many changes in the agencies that are charged with their implementation and the need for increased cooperation among them. Banks should cease to maintain their secrecy and identify their customers and cooperate with law enforcement agencies in reporting suspicious transactions. New forms of analysis, investigation and organisation are required of law enforcement agencies to deal with financial criminal matters.

As noted in Part Two, UK law provides for bank cooperation and the disclosure of suspicious transactions to NCIS; there are now few secure financial havens internationally where the obligation to maintain the confidentiality of bank customers' affairs remains mandatory. Progress in upgrading analytical and investigative capabilities is shown by the growth of the new specialist agencies such as Tracfin (France), Fincen (USA) and Austrac (Australia).

Sources of money laundered funds

The impetus for tackling the money laundering activities of organised crime was inspired originally by an international consensus on the imperative of attacking all aspects of drug-trafficking and capturing drug-trafficking proceeds. At FATF's instigation attempts have been made at a national level to estimate how much criminal money is in circulation and what proportion is drugs derived. In the USA, recent estimates suggest that a third to one half of total illicit proceeds circulating through US financial institutions may be non-drugs proceeds. There are numerous non-drugs crimes to which these proceeds are attributed, notably:

- gambling;
- smuggling;
- pornography;

- loan sharking;
- fraud;
- corruption;
- criminal tax evasion.

Similar trends are noted in Europe. The International Narcotics Control Strategy Report (INCSR) 1994 comments:

> Bankers, finance ministries and enforcement agencies report an apparent increase in non-drug money laundering and seem agreed that drug-related money laundering constitutes no more than three-fourths of the illegal proceeds transferring through or being converted by West European financial institutions (exclusive of tax considerations), and may be at that level or slightly lower in Eastern Europe where large sums of crime syndicate funds are being invested.

Drug money laundering may be no higher, and could be an even lower percentage of total illegal money laundering in other parts of the world, notably Southwest, Southeast and East Asia.

Different countries and regions have different problems with regard to those criminal activities which generate a money laundering demand. North America provides the largest world import market for the product lines of organised crime, such as drugs and illegal immigrants; it is also a major producer and exporter of organised crime in its own right.

The developing regions of South America, Asia and Africa, despite many local differences, are producers and exporters of mainly the following:

Product/service	Examples
organised crime products	cocaine, heroin, methamphetamine
proceeds	Cali cartel bank accounts in Luxembourg
services	Nigerian courier networks
organisations	Chinese triads, Colombian cocaine cartel

Western Europe is both a producer and an exporter and importer of organised crime. As exporters, the Sicilian Mafia have spread their tentacles throughout both Western and Eastern Europe, while maintaining their traditional connections in the United States and elsewhere in the American continents. Conversely, organised crime is imported from the East, primarily from the Russian, Turkish and Chinese mafias, and from Africa, such as the Nigerian groups. There is also a diversity of economic crimes, such as fraud and corruption, of which many are not associated with organised criminal groups.

The non-European criminal organisations which export their products and services to Western Europe, often receive payment through European banking channels. Central and Eastern European countries are potentially major exporters of organised crime in the Russian mould, and seem to provide fields of investment for money laundering by West European criminals.

Reasons for the growth of non-drug related money laundering

The identified growth of non-drug related money, both proportionately and in absolute terms, is probably due to a variety of factors. The most obvious explanation lies in the closer attention which both institutions and governments are giving to criminal money from all significant sources, as a direct result of the representations by international bodies such as FATF and the Council of Europe and of pressure from law enforcement agencies and government departments concerned that anti-drug programmes will not have the same budgetary impact as formerly.

However, Professor Savona, in his September 1994 paper, raised two further possible explanations. First, the proportionate, quantitative expansion of criminal proceeds from non-drug related sources begs the question `whether drug-money accumulation is decreasing or other criminal money is increasing'. Secondly, Professor Savona suggests, it is entirely likely that money laundering schemes used by drug money-launderers have been adopted by professional criminals, particularly organized groups, generally in the process of enhanced professionalism. Thus, the same professional launderers who handle drug money have probably been enlisted, except by those organized groups who handle their own laundering.

Indeed, once the initial process of changing currency notes, which might be identifiable by serial numbers or the residual presence of a drug substance, has been completed, perhaps by a separate exchange professional, there is an advantage for the laundering professional to blend funds from various kinds of criminal transaction in order to obfuscate further any direct association of those funds with a particular drug trafficking source.

Professionalism in money laundering

Partly as a result of the organic development of criminal organisations and partly as a reaction to the new anti-money laundering system and the emphasis on fighting money laundering crime, there is a marked trend towards professionalism in money laundering operations. Evidence that money laundering itself has come of age as a business in its own right is provided by the emergence of two phenomena:

• the increasing involvement in money laundering schemes of financial services professionals, such as private bankers, lawyers and accountants;
• the establishment of money laundering as a business service available to more than one criminal organisation as client and on offer to a wide range of criminals.

Feeding the trend towards professionalism is the growing need for criminal organisations to maximize opportunities and to minimize law enforcement risks. In his paper, Professor Savona identifies three main ways in which organised crime tries to satisfy these requirements:

1. The increasing usage of risk analysis and risk management;
2. The increased usage of technology;

3. Greater professionalism in the cycle of laundering and investment.

Levels of sophistication vary internationally between different
criminal organisations from the use of defence lawyers employed
as house counsel, to the traditional 'consiglieri' in the Mafia
jargon of organized crime and now to the employment of 'risk
analysts' in modern management terminology.

Criminals need to understand the procedural requirements for
law enforcement action in order to minimize risks. For example,
some Colombian drug traffickers hire mainstream American law
firms and defence attorneys to undertake risk analysis and risk
management. Material information that is in public record or
data that are in criminal files released through the process of
trials and courts are studied to evaluate, for instance, how long
it takes the Drugs Enforcement Agency (DEA) or the FBI to
secure a wiretap authorisation, or the local law enforcements
agents in an investigation to process an application for the
wiretap of a particular telephone.

Perhaps the most notorious example of experts' involvement
in the laundering and investment of criminal proceeds through
major institutions is that of the Italian bankers Sindona and Calvi
who worked with the Italian Mafia to launder money on an epic
scale. Likewise, criminal cartels are known to rely heavily on
accountants, many of whom are professionally qualified and
licensed to practice in several countries; they tour the financial
centres of the world frequently to monitor the investments of
their 'clients'.

The language and classification of money laundering services

There is a metaphorical classification for describing the different
levels of money laundering services, such as 'launderette', 'hand-
wash', 'family washing machine' and 'condominium washing
machine', which reflect the professionalism of money laundering
activities.

For example, there are different kinds of 'launderette', of

which some are legitimate mechanisms such as banks and other financial institutions. Sometimes, accredited financial institutions have informal subsidiaries which specialise in money laundering, such as the black network of the notorious Bank of Credit and Commerce International (BCCI).

There are fully or quasi-legitimate alternative systems of informal banking employed extensively by traffickers, such as the Asian hawala or hundi described in Part One. Other alternative mechanisms are the 'casa de cambio' prevalent in Latin America and a whole range of import and export broking firms or brokers of commodities, etc, which may be described loosely as 'private banking structures'.

As Professor Savona and law enforcement practitioners point out, it is often difficult to be sure whether some of these private banking organisations are servicing criminals among their customers or whether the services are also owned by the criminals or criminal organisations. As law enforcement action and the regulation of banking systems becomes more effective, it seems likely that the demand for laundering services in corrupt business for tax evasion and even in official transactions for arms sales etc., as well as for organised crime, is stimulating international alternatives to traditional banking systems. The increasing number of off-shore banks close to drug-producing countries may be construed as evidence of this trend.

Money brokers, who buy cash in bulk at discount rates of around 20 per cent, provide another mechanism for drug traders or other criminals to recover their proceeds from point-of-sale countries without the burden of direct involvement in the laundering process. Although confined to the more sophisticated practitioners of money laundering, such as the Colombian cartels who have been trend-setters traditionally in money laundering, this kind of activity is more common than a few years ago. A more recent phenomenon in the United States is the use of bearer bonds and bearer bond interest coupons as payment consideration for narcotics and a medium of exchange between narcotics dealers.

US government agents, who have had access to records seized through Colombian National Police raids and can also draw on their own investigations, have reported that the Celi cartel which used to handle all money operations internally, now employs financial controllers who seek competitive bids from money brokers; the brokers may process money for more than one drug trafficking organisation at the same time. Not surprisingly, a significant consequence of the document seizures has been that these financial controllers have been driven to use state-of-art communications systems and computer disks in preference to hard copy records.

Not only have the mechanisms for money laundering proliferated; smart criminals are now employing more complex schemes and methods. Frequently criminals decide to 'smurf', the American slang word which describes the technique of dividing a transaction into smaller elements with the use of anonymous helpers to avoid arousing suspicion. At its simplest, the smurf involves placing the proceeds of crime in many banks in order to avoid controls before combining the funds to buy stocks or shares. The banks and the brokerage house provide the mechanism; the smurf is the method. A more complex scheme could involve different methods and mechanisms. The chosen practice of combining or selecting schemes to satisfy the objectives of a criminal organisation form its money laundering strategy.

The main phases of money laundering are called 'placement', 'layering' and 'integration' and may pass through banking and non-bank financial institutions, such as brokerage houses, and through non-financial institutions, such as export brokers.

In spite of the BSA reporting requirements for bankers and the generally high levels of compliance by the financial system with those requirements, many criminals still want their money in regulated financial institutions. They have had to become more creative to insert their criminal proceeds into the financial system, by engaging in more tortuous schemes, often involving the engagement of additional employees.

Collectively, the USA, the UK and Hong Kong have identified the following kinds of non-traditional financial institutions and intermediaries which are involved in various money laundering schemes:

- currency exchanges;
- parallel exchange markets, or 'black' money markets;

- money transmitters;
- securities brokers;
- insurance companies;
- precious metals, stones and artwork dealers/brokers and auction houses;
- casinos/gambling businesses;
- aeroplane, boat, automobile and real estate dealers or brokers.

Although the methods described above suggest that there has been an evolutionary trend from simple money laundering methodology towards a more complex one, the simplest ways of laundering, such as smuggling across borders, persist even today. However, there has been a shift of laundering activity from traditional financial institutions to non-regulated mechanisms where only banks are regulated or to non-financial businesses and mechanisms where both banks and non-bank financial institutions are regulated. Inevitably, the tendency is most marked in the developed countries where more effective anti-money laundering controls are implemented. Indeed, the recent forms of regulation and criminal control are encouraging criminals to move to other less regulated activities.

Professor Ernesto U Savona, from whose paper to the Twelfth International Symposium on Economic Crime at Jesus College, Cambridge from 11 to 17 September much of the material for this and the two succeeding chapters is drawn, is Director, Research Group on Transnational Crime, School of Law, University of Trento,Italy, and Visiting Fellow, National Institute of Justice — US Department of Justice, Washington DC.

3.2
Teeth for Regulators and International Standards of Practice

Jonathan Reuvid

In Chapter 3.1 the main goals of government anti-money laundering policies were identified as attacking criminal activities, particularly those of organised crime, and as defending the transparency of the economic and financial systems. The second goal is the prerequisite for protecting the integrity of the financial systems and is discussed in the next chapter.

Effective control of organised crime demands strong and cohesive legislation on a national basis which is mutually consistent internationally within regulatory frameworks such as the Council of Europe 1991 Convention on the Laundering of the Proceeds of Crime and, at the least, a coordinated set of domestic, regional and international mechanisms based on a common anti-laundering system of soft laws. Much of this has been achieved in the regions and countries where the 40 FATF recommendations have been adopted and there is a high level of cooperation between law enforcement agencies in tracking criminal proceeds and pooling information. However, the common anti-money laundering provisions of the present regulatory system need to be almost universal in order to be fully effective against international criminals. Criminal organisations are adept at shifting the scope and direction of their illegal activities to the products and channels where the detection capability of law enforcement agencies is weakest and to countries where legislation against economic crime is less complete.

Therefore, in terms of crime prevention, the first objective in any country must be to enhance the 'law enforcement risk' for criminals. This all-embracing term includes both the risk of being identified, arrested and convicted, the 'apprehension risk' and the risk that the proceeds of crime will be forfeited, the 'confiscation risk'. There will be a great disincentive to incur the risk of generating illicit proceeds if the apprehension risk is increased and, at the same time, it becomes more difficult for criminals to retain the proceeds of their crimes.

In fact, for organised crime, the confiscation risk may be a more effective deterrent than the apprehension risk. A criminal organisation with a hierarchical structure which places emphasis on continuity can control the 'apprehension risk' by planned over-staffing or effective replacement procedures, accompanied by sufficient layers of organisation, financial rewards and a reputation for violence which will minimize the likelihood of an arrested member jeopardising the future of the group through disclosure. Organisations like the Triads, the Mafia and the Boryokudan have demonstrated their ability to survive the imprisonment of individual members without serious damage to profitability.

However, all these defence mechanisms are ineffective against the damage resulting from confiscation of criminal proceeds which impacts profitability and frustrates the objectives of both criminals individually and of criminal organisations. Forcing organised crime to work harder and take greater risk for less return is an effective economic disincentive. The various measures, described in Chapter 2.2, taken to facilitate the confiscation of criminal proceeds in one country arising from the commitment of a crime in another country provide the backbone to this approach.

Money laundering's significance to law enforcement lies in the ability of a government to fight organised crime, not only through prosecution of profit-generating activity but by causing havoc financially to international criminal enterprises through the confiscation of assets derived from money laundering. Confiscated drugs are easily replaceable by continued cultivation and processing, but the accumulated proceeds from drug production and trafficking and assets acquired subsequently are altogether harder to replace after confiscation.

The growing internationalisation of organised crime is a fact of life and reflects, in part, the more complex schemes used. It may be the outcome of new transnational dimensions of criminal organisations operating on a global market, for example, selling cocaine in Europe as well as in North America or buying heroin from Mexico rather than from Southeast Asia when the price and quality offer improved prospects for better resale profits. Internationalisation in money laundering schemes may also be a deliberate strategy to take advantage of imperfect investigative cooperation, a lack of harmonization between domestic legislations, bank secrecy, absence of regulation etc in those countries constituting the weak links in the global anti-money laundering chain.

It follows that the response to this increasing complexity in money laundering activities which use unregulated mechanisms, has been:

- a demand for the regulation of non-bank financial institutions;
- demands on national legislators, law enforcement agencies and criminal justice systems inviting them to adapt their domestic legislations to the FATF recommendations and to implement them widely.

Extending the anti-money laundering system internationally

Simultaneously in many regions and countries, guided by North America and Western Europe, the process of adapting international legal norms and the establishment of new financial regulations and criminal legislation is pressing forward. While Eastern European countries have begun to address the system relatively recently, South America is following North American and Western European practice, albeit without uniformity.

Few African countries have developed anti-money laundering policies. The problem of implementing the various anti-money laundering policies at domestic levels is probably greater than the problem of harmonizing legislation. Practice in Asian countries varies between extremes. Some countries act intensively against money laundering; in many others officials deliberate ignore money laundering by criminals.

The effectiveness and efficiency of domestic systems, where they have been created, is a subject for continuing discussion. The differences among countries in their efforts to prevent and control money laundering reduce the effectiveness of the whole system. Criminals search out the countries where the risk that their money will be traced and confiscated is less and investments are more productive, as a part of their strategy of moving money rapidly and increasing the return on their investments. Therefore, domestic anti-money laundering systems and the international system are interdependent with the effectiveness of the one closely connected to the effectiveness of the other. An effective anti-money laundering strategy relies upon the successful combination of domestic policies controlling the placement of criminal proceeds and the harmonization of policies among all countries to equalize the risk for criminals.

Making domestic and international anti-money laundering systems effective

For anti-money laundering systems to be effective domestically and internationally, it is clear that in each country both regulatory and crime control policies must be established according to some minimum common criteria which set an international standard for the intensity with which the policies are pursued. To achieve this result, an integrated system of international cooperation must be realised and international mechanisms, such as banks, and countries should solicit and help other countries to participate in a common protective net based on recognised criteria. This is the stated goal of recent international money laundering conferences.

It is widely recognised that cooperation among banks and financial institutions with law enforcement agencies requires regulation to be fully effective and cannot be achieved on a voluntary basis only. However, cooperation cannot be compelled and, as Professor Savona comments in his September 1994 Cambridge paper, 'It needs a degree of motivation that exceeds the resistance against it'.

To achieve effective cooperation worldwide, it is clear that the establishment in more countries of new agencies along the lines of Fincen in the USA and Tracfin in France, where law enforcement skills are allied to banking expertise through multi-discipline staff, would help greatly to achieve a solution. In addition, Professor Savona suggests that an organisational analysis of law enforcement agencies, of banking and the financial industry should be undertaken which would identify inter alia incentives to cooperate and disincentives to engage in corrupt behaviour. Incentives for law enforcement agencies, for example, could be of an economic nature, such as sharing seized criminal assets or career rewards for those engaged in the financial investigation area.

A further necessary condition for an effective and efficient anti-money laundering system is the maintenance of a high level of flexibility in the system. Organised crime is very flexible in exploiting loopholes in banking and financial systems for their money laundering activities. Recognising the effectiveness of a particular control system, criminals will contrive to avoid it. Thus, a system for controlling money laundering which has been effective for some time may become obsolete overnight, and rapid adjustments to the system are required.

Progress in these directions can be made only if the development of an effective international money laundering policy is placed on the agendas of countries worldwide and the issue retains a high profile among government regulators and legislators.

3.3
Protecting the Integrity of the Financial System

Jonathan Reuvid

The second, more defensive objective of governments in pursuing their anti-money laundering policies is to protect the transparency and integrity of the economic and financial systems.

Criminal money has serious effects on economic and financial systems:

- It distorts competition in the market place. Legitimate money, on which taxes are paid has an investment cost which is higher than criminal money and cannot compete effectively against low cost criminal proceeds.
- It creates political advantages making it easier for criminal organisations to infiltrate 'respectable' straw men representing them into political and economic affairs.

Of the three sets of 40 FATF recommendations, the second referred to under the heading of 'Enhancement of the Role of the Financial System' refers to the policy of making the financial systems more transparent. The first and third sets of FATF recommendations grouped under the headings 'The Improvement of National Legal Systems to Combat Money Laundering' and 'Strengthening of International Cooperation' support the first, more aggressive objective of attacking criminal activities and have been discussed in the previous two chapters.

Essentially, the objective of penal deterrence or control is addressed by criminal legislation and administration, whereas financial transparency and integrity is pursued through the exercise of regulatory powers. However, the two objectives are closely connected with the interaction between the two remedies. Criminal penalties are often applied to reinforce the integrity or transparency of the financial system, while regulatory policies are used to detect or deter criminal activities.

We have already noted in Part Two how law enforcement authorities seek to enlist the help of banks and bank regulators in identifying and tracing observed flows of criminal proceeds through regulated financial institutions with banks in the UK, for example, mandated to report suspicious cash transfers and transactions to NCIS.

Conversely, customer identification requirements which are typically regulatory obligations of bank and non-bank financial institutions, are strengthened by administrative and criminal penalties for the non-complying financial institution officer, as well as for the customer who is in violation of those require-ments eg by submitting false identity documents.

Motivation for banks and financial institutions to cooperate with law enforcement agencies

The main motivation for banks and financial institutions to cooperate with law enforcers is based on the maintenance of repu-tation. Operating in highly competitive markets, they value their reputations highly and the majority of the customers whom they serve, at least those who are legitimate, demand that the banks and financial institutions with whom they deal are not involved in frauds or other economic crimes. Corporate sanctions against banks who transgress are not only an economic deterrent; they also detract from reputation.

The restoration of reputation, as we have seen recently in the case of Barings, Britain's oldest and one of its most prestigious banks, is a painful process. The uncontrolled activities of one derivatives trader in Singapore generated surprise mega-losses of such a magnitude that the parent company was thrown into temporary receivership, from which it was rescued rapidly by the Dutch bank Internationale Nederlander Group. However, this prompt action was insufficient to restore confidence among corporate clients and the financial community at large. In the aftermath of the débâcle, and pending the outcome of a protracted Bank of England investigation, it was necessary for the new owner to demand the resignation of some 20 senior managers in London, Singapore and Tokyo, effectively all those within whose remit and under whose responsibility, direct or remote, the rogue trader had operated. Issues of complicity, misfeasance, misrepresentation, negligence and incompetence were unclarified at the time and no personal blame had been assigned publicly. It remains to be seen whether such draconian action, implying managerial failure by association will be effective in restoring market confidence in Barings' international securities trading business.

Another aspect of the relationship between banks and other financial institutions with law enforcement agencies and the entire anti-money laundering system is the cost burden on banks of competing with reporting procedures. In effect, the achievement of transparency can reduce the efficiency of financial systems so that competition between banks and financial systems having these costly controls and banks and financial systems of countries which tolerate, or even enforced banking secrecy is unequal. Since criminal operators search out locations where banking secrecy is high, the only way to attack criminal organisations and promote transparency simultaneously is to harmonise equal criteria for both controls and transparency between countries worldwide. Investigations into the Bank of Credit and Commerce International (BCCI) confirmed how the international payments system was utilised by money laundering networks and demonstrated the need to modify bank secrecy laws so that responses to investigating law enforcement agencies may be coordinated internationally.

The integrity of the financial system internationally is under threat in other respects. The fraudulent banking of BCCI and the Baring Securities saga in the UK and a number of irregularities and misadventures on Wall Street in the securities operations of leading US investment houses call into question the adequacy of internal audit systems and of the controls applied by the regulatory authorities in leading financial centres.

In the UK, the Bank of England is responsible for the monitoring of all domestic banking operations, investigating suspected irregularities and applying sanctions where an individual bank is in breach of its rules or codes of practice. In the USA, the Securities Exchange Commission (SEC) has a federal responsibility to monitor all securities' transactions, companies whose securities are exchanged in any of the markets within its remit and applications for listing. The SEC has statutory powers to investigate, apply sanctions and instigate prosecution where appropriate.

The difference in emphasis between statutory regulation in the US and self-regulation in the UK is traditional with British financial institutions strongly favouring the latter. However, in the post-Big Bang era of the 1980s and 1990s self-regulation has been woefully wanting in the UK securities industry and in the London insurance market where the integrity of Lloyd's of London and its underwriting syndicates have been under intense public scrutiny. The adverse effects on reputation arising from failure to regulate financial institutions and their behaviour have been more severe than the impact of organised criminal operations.

3.4
Improved Auditing Practice

Martyn E Jones

One of the key ways of minimising the potential for losses arising from economic crime is the application of auditing techniques. Such auditing techniques can be applied as part of the organisation's control framework when they form part of activities described as internal audit, inspection or monitoring. They can also be applied by external auditors or forensic accountants.

Traditional auditing techniques, such as testing transactions to supporting documentation, are, however, becoming less successful at detecting fraud. This is because of:

- the use of office technology which makes forgery of documents easier;
- the increasing complexity of transactions and financial instruments eg derivatives
- the growth of information technology which makes manual supervision of staff and transactions less effective than hitherto;
- the growth of 'havens of secrecy';
- the increased speed of transactions.

The result is that the playing field is increasingly being tilted in favour of the fraudster. The purpose of this article is to describe some steps which can be taken to improve the effectiveness of audit in relation to detecting and preventing economic crime.

1. Begin at the top. Ensure that the main reporting lines for auditors flow via an audit committee which includes non-executive directors. Suggest that a review take place of the

control environment (take note of the material on internal control issued by COSO in the US, Cadbury in the UK and COCO in Canada.

2. Think risk. Encourage the identification and prioritisation of critical business and financial risk. Consider carefully the nature of the industry and determine where the organisation and its competitors have suffered losses before. History frequently repeats itself and it is the best indicator of future frauds and irregularities.

3. Prioritise and plan the areas to be covered by audit. Focus mainly on the high risk areas and make sure there is an element of surprise.

4. Consider the organisation's control objectives and the under-lying considerations taking account of relevant benchmarks which currently include: IT – the standards issued by the EDPAA, and derivatives – the recommendation of the US Group of Thirty.
   Control environment, identification of risk, monitoring, information and communication, and control procedures – COSO, Cadbury and COCO.

5. Arrange for a 'culture review'. The people or places within the system where fraud occurs are frequently fairly predictable. Identify the features which can be used to diagnose such people or places. Focus on staff who display wealth, have been rapidly promoted probably above their abilities, positions where there is a history of fraud, and positions where staff have access to large sums of money but are paid very little.

6. Focus attention on transactions with related parties (ie with relatives or management or other entities owned by them) or which involve payments to or from havens of secrecy.

7. Aim to create a culture which makes economic crime as difficult as possible to perpetrate. Recommend codes of conduct, performance indicators to identify units and locations which are out of line, and proper vetting of people hired to positions of trust. Ensure that audit evidence is as reli-

able as possible. Look at whether printers and valuable stationery are susceptible to alteration and fraud. Arrange for a rule which makes it a serious disciplinary offence to knowingly mislead an internal auditor. Lobby for change in the law to make knowingly misleading an external auditor a criminal offence resulting in a custodial sentence.

8. Make use of IT based techniques such as risk evaluation packages, file interrogation techniques and electronic recording. If cost is an obstacle, minimise the 'mountain of paper' traditionally associated with auditing. Train staff to pull together in one place all points for further review. Do not expect reviewers to have to glean through the detail to find significant points which have been tucked away on an insignificant looking paper.

9. Develop a reporting methodology which emphasises succinctness, prioritisation of conclusions and recommended next steps rather than 'long turgid text', treating all points as equal and vague general conclusions. Remember that people at the top have very limited time and that they prefer short, focused, structured reports rather than long rambling reports.

10. Be aware of the principles of gathering legal evidence and involve those with a relevant forensic background when developing a case against someone suspected of economic crime. Report only when one is sure of one's facts.

11. Recognise that good audit practice depends on the development of relevant knowledge. Don't assume that audit staff will find fraud especially when they are untrained and the symptoms of industry specific frauds to which the organisation may be exposed have not been defined. Develop ways of sharing the ideas of the best auditors with others and when auditors retire make sure that their wisdom is not lost by recording and sharing their best tips and hints.

Unfortunately, given the nature of temptation, fraud will never be eliminated. Auditing is therefore a vocation which needs to be as strong as possible in order to make life for the potential fraudster as hard as possible.

3.5
Corporate Governance*

Martyn E Jones

*The author and the publishers gratefully acknowledge the Committee on the Financial Aspects of Corporate Governance and Gee and Co Ltd for permitting unrestricted publication of the Code of Best Practice.

If one analyses many of the spectacular economic crimes that stem from weaknesses in corporate governance, or the way in which business are managed and controlled, recurring patterns can be recognised. These weaknesses include:

- the dominant chief executive with unfettered powers who has difficulty in distinguishing between personal assets and those of the company;
- insufficient checks and balances over the executive directors;
- lack of a clear role for the board of directors and for non-executive directors;
- inadequate control over the levels of executive remuneration;
- insufficient disclosure of what is actually happening to the business.

Of course it is always easy with hindsight to identify what was wrong 'at the top'. What matters most is to take the lessons from what has happened in the past and to change the framework of management and control over business so as to reduce the possibility for economic crime. By shedding some light on developments in recent years in the United Kingdom, a template for other countries to follow may be suggested.

A growing crisis of confidence in business (and in particular the way it was managed and audited) grew in the wake of a recession in the late 1980s and early 1990s. Too many companies suddenly failed including Polly Peck, the Maxwell companies and their pension scheme, and BCCI. Action was needed to prevent the reputation of the UK as a financial and business centre being severely damaged. The response came from a large number of bodies (including the Stock Exchange, the Law Society and the accountancy profession) which with the support of the government, set up a committee to review the financial aspects of corporate governance. The committee needed a chairman and were fortunate when Sir Adrian Cadbury, a very experienced and respected industrialist, was appointed. The 'Cadbury' era then began.

The Committee set up in May 1991, began by seeking the view of anyone who was interested in corporate governance. All sorts of ideas were considered. The German system of having a management board with a supervisory board above it was considered but rejected as too radical a change. A draft report was issued for comment, and in December 1992 after the Committee considered that a consensus had been reached the Report of the Committee on the Financial Aspects of Corporate Governance (the Cadbury Report) was published.

Many people had high expectations. Some, who believed that change was unnecessary for their companies, probably hoped that like many official reports this one would gather dust and be forgotten. They were wrong. A very clever knot had been tied. Issued with the Report was a brief Code. Listed and unlisted securities market companies incorporated in the UK were for part or whole periods ending after 30 June 1993 required to make a statement in their report and accounts about their compliance with the Code and to identify and give their reasons for any areas of non-compliance. These statements were also required to be reviewed by auditors to the extent that they could be objectively verified. In addition (and to the surprise of some) a publication of statement of compliance, reviewed by the auditors, was made a continuation obligation of listing by the London Stock Exchange. The Code is set out below.

The Code of Best Practice

1 The Board of Directors

1.1 The board should meet regularly, retain full and effective control over the company and monitor the executive management.

1.2 There should be a clearly accepted division of responsibilities at the head of a company, which will ensure a balance of power and authority, such that no one individual has unfettered powers of decision. Where the chairman is also the chief executive, it is essential that there should be a strong and independent element on the board, with a recognised senior member.

1.3 The board should include non-executive directors of sufficient calibre and number for their views to carry significant weight in the board's decisions. (Note 1)

1.4 The board should have a formal schedule of matters specifically reserved to it for decision to ensure that the direction and control of the company is firmly in its hands. (Note 2)

1.5 There should be an agreed procedure for directors in the furtherance of their duties to take independent professional advice if necessary, at the company's expense. (Note 3)

1.6 All directors should have access to the advice and services of the company secretary, who is responsible to the board for ensuring that board procedures are followed and that applicable rules and regulations are complied with. Any question of the removal of the company secretary should be a matter for the board as a whole.

2 Non-Executive Directors

2.1 Non-executive directors should bring an independent judgement to bear on issues of strategy, performance, resources, including key appointments, and standards of conduct.

2.2 The majority should be independent of management and free from any business or other relationship which could materially interfere with the exercise of their independent judgement, apart from their fees and shareholding. Their fees should reflect the time which they commit to the company. (Notes 4 and 5)

2.3 Non-executive directors should be appointed for specified terms and re-appointment should not be automatic. (Note 6)

2.4 Non-executive directors should be selected through a formal process and both this process and their appointment should be a matter for the board as a whole. (Note 7)

3 Executive Directors

3.1 Directors' service contracts should not exceed three years without shareholders' approval. (Note 8)

3.2 There should be full and clear disclosure of directors' total emoluments and those of the chairman and highest-paid UK director, including pension contributions and stock options. Separate figures should be given for salary and performance-related elements and the basis on which performance is measured should be explained.

3.3 Executive directors' pay should be subject to the recommendations of a remuneration committee made up wholly or mainly of non-executive directors. (Note 9)

4 Reporting and Controls

4.1 It is the board's duty to present a balanced and understandable assessment of the company's position. (Note 10)

4.2 The board should ensure that an objective and professional relationship is maintained with the auditors.

4.3 The board should establish an audit committee of at least three non-executive directors with written terms of reference which deal clearly with its authority and duties. (Note 11)

4.4 The directors should explain their responsibility for preparing the accounts next to a statement by the auditors about their reporting responsibilities. (Note 12)

4.5 The directors should report on the effectiveness of the company's system of internal control. (Note 13)

4.6 The directors should report that the business is a going concern, with supporting assumptions or qualifications as necessary. (Note 13)

Notes

These notes include further recommendations on good practice. They do not form part of the Code.

1   To meet the Committee's recommendations on the composition of sub-committees of the board, boards will require a minimum of three non-executive directors, one of whom may be the chairman of the company provided he or she is not also its executive head. Additionally, two of the three non-executive directors should be independent in the terms set out in paragraph 2.2 of the Code.

2   A schedule of matters specifically reserved for decision by the full board should be given to directors on appointment and should be kept up to date. The Committee envisages that the schedule would at least include:

(a)   acquisition and disposal of assets of the company or its subsidiaries that are material to the company

(b)   investments, capital projects, authority levels, treasury policies and risk management policies.

The board should lay down rules to determine materiality for any transaction, and should establish clearly which transactions require multiple board signatures. The board should also agree the procedures to be followed when, exceptionally, decisions are required between board meetings.

3   The agreed procedure should be laid down formally, for example in a Board Resolution, in the Articles, or in the Letter of Appointment.

4   It is for the board to decide in particular cases whether this definition of independence is met. Information about the relevant interests of directors should be disclosed in the Directors' Report.

5   The Committee regards it as good practice for non-executive directors not to participate in share option schemes and for their service as non-executive directors not to be pensionable by the company, in order to safeguard their independent position.

6   The Letter of Appointment for non-executive directors should set out their duties, term of office, remuneration, and its

review.

7   The Committee regards it as good practice for a nomination committee to carry out the selection process and to
make proposals to the board. A nomination committee
should have a majority of non-executive directors on it and
be chaired either by the chairman or a non-executive director.

8   The Committee does not intend that this provision should
apply to existing contracts before they become due for
renewal.

9   Membership of the remuneration committee should be set
out in the Directors' Report and its chairman should be
available to answer questions on remuneration principles and
practice at the Annual General Meeting. Best practice is set
out in PRO NED's Remuneration Committee guidelines,
published in 1992. (Available at the price of £5 from PRO
NED, 1 Kingsway, London WC2B 6XF, telephone 0171
240 8305.)

10   The report and accounts should contain a coherent narra-
tive, supported by the figures, of the company's performance and prospects. Balance requires that setbacks should
be dealt with as well as successes. The need for the report
to be readily understood emphasises that words are as
important as figures.

11   The Committee's recommendations on audit committees are
as follows:

(a) They should be formally constituted as sub-committees of
the main board to whom they are answerable and to whom
they should report regularly; they should be given written
terms of reference which deal adequately with their membership, authority and duties; and they should normally meet
at least twice a year.

(b) There should be a minimum of three members. Membership
should be confined to the non-executive directors of the
company and a majority of the non-executives serving on
the committee should be independent of the company, as
defined in paragraph 2.2 of the Code.

(c) The external auditor and, where an internal audit function
exists, the head of internal audit should normally attend
committee meetings, as should the finance director. Other

board members should also have the right to attend.

(d) The audit committee should have a discussion with the auditors at least once a year, without executive board members present, to ensure that there are no unresolved issues of concern.

(e) The audit committee should have explicit authority to investigate any matters within its terms of reference, the resources which it needs to do so, and full access to information. The committee should be able to obtain outside professional advice and if necessary to invite outsiders with relevant experience to attend meetings.

(f) Membership of the committee should be disclosed in the annual report and the chairman of the committee should be available to answer questions about its work at the Annual General Meeting.

Specimen terms of reference for an audit committee, including a list of the most commonly performed duties, are set out in the Committee's full report.

12 The statement of directors' responsibilities should cover the following points:

- the legal requirement for directors to prepare financial statements for each financial year which give a true and fair view of the state of affairs of the company (or group) as at the end of the financial year and of the profit and loss for that period;

- the responsibility of the directors for maintaining adequate accounting records, for safeguarding the assets of the company (or group), and for preventing and detecting fraud and other irregularities;

- confirmation that suitable accounting policies, consistently applied and supported by reasonable and prudent judgements and estimates, have been used in the preparation of the financial statements;

- confirmation that applicable accounting standards have been followed, subject to any material departures disclosed and explained in the notes to the accounts. (This does not obviate the need for a formal statement in the notes to the accounts disclosing whether the accounts have been prepared in accordance with applicable accounting standards).

The statement should be placed immediately before the auditors' report which in future will include a separate statement (currently being developed by the Auditing Practices Board) on the responsibility of the auditors for expressing an opinion on the accounts.

13 The Committee notes that companies will not be able to comply with paragraphs 4.5 and 4.6 of the Code until the necessary guidance for companies has been developed as recommended in the Committee's report.

14 The company's statement of compliance should be reviewed by the auditors in so far as it relates to paragraphs 1.4, 1.5, 2.3, 2.4, 3.1 to 3.3, and 4.3 to 4.6 of the Code.

The response has been dramatic. A survey which Touche Ross & Co conducted on the annual report and accounts of the FT-SE 100 companies (ie the 100 largest companies) issued between 1 January and 31 May 1994 revealed that all the companies surveyed included a statement of compliance with the Code. Of the 55 companies which issued annual reports and accounts in that period 52 indicated compliance with all operative provisions of the Code and only three stated that they did not comply with the Code.

Behind the scenes much has happened to bring about this situation. Non-executive directors were appointed, sub-committee on directors' remuneration and for audit were established, some companies split the role of the chairman and chief executive and in many companies the system of checks and balances has been improved.

This is not to say that financial scandals will disappear but hopefully they will be less likely to arise in future. Much work still remains and at the time of writing the remaining parts of the Code to become operative (reporting on the going concern basis and on the system of financial control) are being finalised. Board rooms will however be open to greater scrutiny and the investing public will have criteria to judge whether a business has an adequate corporate governance framework. A regime of more openness will encourage good practice and discourage bad practice.

Clearly the UK model may not be the solution for all other countries but it could serve as a useful basis for emerging economic states (and individual business within such states) to set the right tone at the top.

3.6
The Mobilisation of Public Opinion

Sir Kenneth Warren

In this century public and private wealth have boomed. The benefits have flowed from the 'first world' into the 'second world'. The principal motive power has been science. Discoveries, turned into technologies, have spawned new industries, new ways of business and wider dimensions of opportunity.

Energy resources – carbon based and nuclear – have been the founding base for whole new global industries: aerospace, electronics, chemicals and pharmaceuticals. The communications revolution in aerospace and telecommunications, the ability to move people and data with ease, has transformed financial services into a business taking less than a second to circle the world with information. Even bureaucracy has blossomed as governments have tapped the greater wealth, and so gained more and more power over all of us.

The traditional battle between the entrepreneur wanting freedom in the market-place, and those wanting equity in competition, has spilled over from single nation states into the world as a single market, with men of stated goodwill in governments banding together to protect the citizens they represent. The United Nations, the World Bank, the International Monetary Fund, the World Health Organisation, the European Union, all regulate internationally with 'repeaters' in every nation regulating everything in the names of perceived logic and common sense.

But another, unwelcome business boom has sounded across the 20th century. The creation and accumulation of wealth, coupled with 'Regulation', has attracted crime on to the international stage. The simplicity achieved in communications has added to their importance in every form of transaction. What is intended to be for the sole benefit of people of probity, automatically attracts people of lesser qualities ever eager to 'hack' into business transmissions and circumvent regulations installed as protection for the public.

Nobody knows the dimensions of international crime. 'Old Masters', flash cars, glittering jewels can be selected and stolen to order, and be abroad before a loss is discovered.

Nobody knows how many computer data bases are tapped. Too many business people are still in the 'Can't happen here' camp. Computer security, even at NATO HQs, has been found to have been breached by professional spies and by amateur hackers.

The centralisation of power, so popular in board rooms and even more so in government, is a magnet for the criminal as strong as a light to a moth. The difference is that the criminal recognises the risk. To penetrate a power base such as a bank, a government organisation or a business with a commodity in demand, readily traded – from arms to drugs, from clothes designs to crops – requires bright brains. The 'killings' can be and are known to be huge, from whole tankers filled with oil simply disappearing – and their crews as well – to the rigging of stock markets and the dreadful destruction of human life wrought by drug dealers.

Every year since 1983 the International Symposium of Economic Crime has been convened at Jesus College, Cambridge. Every year bizarre but true tales are recounted by the 250 delegates from across the world about the spread of 'white-collar' crime. One constant theme is that the forces of the law are always behind and never in front of the stormtroopers of criminality. But the liaison gets better each year between the law-enforcers. After 12 Symposia the law-makers are all too noticeable by their continuing absence. They are failing to learn from international experience about an international horror.

Catching and depriving criminals of their gains is a cause which never lacks public support. But visible success is the essential sight required by the public, under attack and paying for its own protection. Governments and international organisations are continually organising and reorganising the barriers to theft. A panoply of devices are used: the creation and updating of laws, trans-national agreements on extradition of suspects and criminals, the seizing of assets, the capture of illegal profits. It is now universally recognised by law-enforcers that much more attention is required to setting up and maintaining civil and administrative enforcement actions to common international standards.

Progress is being made, but progress is too slow. For instance, Spain, once a sunny refuge for men our own police were anxious 'to help them with their enquiries', has accepted it has obligations as a member of the European Union to other member states. Brazil, the refuge of a Mr Ronnie Biggs, whom our domestic authorities would also like to meet again on home ground, still wavers; but Mr Biggs' son, when 18 years old, is expected to be told by the Brazilian government that he does not need his father's protection any more, thus enabling his father to put him on a plane to London. These two cases illustrate the failure of politicians to act across borders in their mutual interests.

But whereas some nation states may be eager to collaborate with others where criminals are concerned, they are not necessarily as understanding as may be wished, where theft can involve intellectual property – designs and patents. In recent years Russia, Taiwan and other Pacific Rim countries including the People's Republic of China, have been the target of countries seeking the due to their own inventors and designers through the granting and regulation of protection of intellectual property. Progress is being made, but Polo and Dior menswear in the markets of Thailand is still only a quarter of the price charged on the Champs Elysee or Fifth Avenue. Good copies of Gucci, Piaget and Rolex watches are sold to tourists for less than £7, just below the counters in Bangkok, or Taipei. No guarantees are available.

Which brings up the question, where does international crime, particularly financial fraud begin? The tempted tourist and the 'Godfather' are partners in crime. Yet the English farmer growing linseed nobody wants, under European Union subsidy rules, is carrying on his business absolutely legally. He is paid over £400 a hectare for a crop costing less than half that to produce before it is dumped. The German farmer, growing tobacco which will not ripen, likewise is carrying on his business absolutely legally.

With his Euro-cousins in Italy and Greece (where tobacco does ripen, but nobody in Europe will smoke it), he shares out £750 million a year in subsidies. And the suggestion is about that some farmers around the Mediterranean may not grow as many hectares of tobacco as they claim – rather like the question of the olive groves which appear and then disappear.

Fraud in the European Union is believed to be costing Euro-taxpayers billions and billions of pounds, francs, marks and lire each year. Organised crime, not just slightly sly agricultural industry producers, processors and salesmen, is known to be hard at work and doing very well indeed.

Indeed, where bureaucracy and big money meet, organised crime is never far behind. A perfect example of where the interests of politicians and organised crime can meet, to the detriment of the former and the probable benefit to the latter, is staring us in the face. With the updating and revision of the 1957 Treaty of Rome scheduled for an inter-governmental conference, the 'IGA' in 1996, there needs to be massive public and political pressure to bring into the machinery of the Union the missing quality of accountability essential for the proper working of the Brussels bureaucracy. The current lack of this necessary accountability makes the Euro-system a wonderful target for international crime.

Whereas the founding fathers in 1957 appeared to assume, in the construction of the EEC, that democracy would rule automatically; the impossibility of this became self-evident as the bureaucrats of Brussels found that the Council of Ministers and an emasculated European Assembly, later labelled a 'parliament', could not possibly cope with the complexity of the business which had to be completed to meet the ideals and Articles of the Treaty of Rome. Thus bureaucrats were forced to take over, and the resulting deluge of Directives and Regulations showered on the 250 million citizens of the EU are well-intentioned, but not the output of a democratic process as originally intended.

Much good has been achieved, particularly in financial services; banking, insurance and quality assurance of international transactions. But 'money laundering' of the proceeds of fraud against the European Union and on behalf of the drug cartels is still too easy. Combatting fraud requires global controls. Perfection will be impossible to achieve, but political leadership at the level of the OECD countries, let alone the United Nations, is running far behind public requirements. For instance the Court of Auditors, sponsored by the UK, in the European Union, is only an innovation of recent years. It is underfunded and under-staffed. One is forced to wonder why some members of the EU give the strong impression of reluctance to support the Court.

Bring together financial services, good electronic communication and an overloaded bureaucracy, and problems are inevitable. Every law, every regulation ever devised has a loophole, a caveat, a deficiency, or a reason to be ignored; sometimes all of these. Then adding financial penalties and rewards to encourage compliance makes lawyers and criminals, in unintended paradoxical association, rich. And whereas lawyers never employ criminals, the reverse is traditional in organised crime.

Presumably the IGA in 1996 is intended to be the formula for the next 40 years for the European Union. Politicians have got little time and much work to do. International crime is hoping the time available will not be found and work will be left undone. Political failure will be their reward and the peoples' lasting misfortune.

The quality of the example which will be set by the European Union will be watched by the world. In turn, therefore, world standards in financial dealings will be locked in to Europe's achievement, or Europe's failure. London, the financial centre of the EU, ranks with New York and is ahead of Tokyo as a centre of business excellence. Financial success does not sell newspapers as well as financial malfeasance. In combatting the international financial criminal fraternity a sense of proportion that all is not bad is essential. But public awareness of the dangers has yet to be raised by the media and the politicians to a level equivalent to that which the public needs to understand. After all, it is their money.

Appendix I

(An extract from United Kingdom Guidelines on international mutual legal assistance in criminal matters, issued by the UK Central Authority, August 1991.)

Contents of Requests for Mutual Assistance

Requests for assistance should contain:

(a) details of the authority making the request

(b) details of the purpose of the request and a summary of the reason for it

(c) details of persons named in the request (full names, places and dates of birth, known addresses, nationality, etc)

(d) a description of the offences or suspected offences charged or likely to be charged or under investigation

(e) any relevant dates (eg date of trial) or cause for special urgency (eg where the accused is in detention pending the investigation of his or her case)

(f) in the case of a request for search and seizure, full details of the property to be seized, and other information necessary to satisfy the requirements shown in paragraphs 26-34 below

(g) in the case of a request for the freezing or confiscation of criminal assets, the information and documents indicated in the applicable bilateral confiscation agreement or side letter (see Annex D)

(h) in the case of a request for the attendance of a witness abroad, details of allowances and travelling and subsistence expenses payable by the requesting State

(i) details of any rules on privilege which a witness or suspect may be entitled to claim, and any caution which should if possible be given under the law of the requesting State

(j)   where evidence is to be taken from a witness or suspect, details of whether the evidence is to be taken before a court, and whether it should be taken on oath or affirmation; alternatively, confirmation that a less formal interview not on oath, for example by the police, will suffice. (In the absence of such indication or confirmation the Central Authority may use its discretion)

(k)   a description of the evidence sought, and a list of any specific questions to be asked

(l)   where the evidence is to be taken before a court, certification should be provided by the authority forwarding the request to the Central Authority to the effect that there are reasonable grounds for suspecting that an offence has been committed, and either that proceedings in respect of the offence have been instituted or that an investigation is being carried out within its jurisdiction

(m)   whether it is desired that any persons from the requesting State should be present during the taking of evidence, and whether the request is for such persons to be permitted to participate in the questioning. (See paragraph 23 below)

(n)   in the case of a prisoner witness required abroad, information will be needed to enable the prisoner's informed consent to be sought and to satisfy the UK prison authorities that arrangements will be made to ensure his or her secure custody. This information will need to include details of proposed arrangements for collecting the prisoner from the United Kingdom; details of the type of secure accommodation in which he or she will be held in the requesting State; the type of escort to and from his or her accommodation; the period during which attendance in the requesting State is required; the date on which the court or other proceedings for which the prisoner is required will commence, and are likely to be concluded; the privileges (letters, visits, etc) to which the prisoner will be entitled during his or her attendance in the requesting State, and whether he or she will be accorded immunity in respect of previous offences. Further information regarding the requirements for transfer of particular prisoners may be sought from the Central Authority.

Appendix II

Ratification of 1988 Convention Against Illicit Traffic in Narcotic Drugs and Psychotropic Substances

1	Bahamas	30 January 1989
2	China	25 October 1989
3	Senegal	27 November 1989
4	Bahrain	7 February 1990
5	USA	20 February 1990
6	Chile	13 March 1990
7	Ecuador	23 March 1990
8	India (Accession)	27 March 1990
9	Ghana	10 April 1990
10	Mexico	11 April 1990
11	UAE	12 April 1990
12	Jordan	16 April 1990
13	Nicaragua	4 May 1990
14	Qatar (Accession)	4 May 1990
15	Cyprus	25 May 1990
16	Canada	5 July 1990
17	Togo	1 August 1990
18	Spain	13 August 1990
19	Bolivia	20 August 1990
20	Uganda	20 August 1990
21	Paraguay	23 August 1990
22	Bhutan (Accession)	27 August 1990
23	Tunisia	20 September 1990
24	Bangladesh	11 October 1990
25	Grenada	10 December 1990
26	Russian Federation	17 December 1990
27	Guinea (Accession)	27 December 1990
28	Italy (Approval)	31 December 1990

29	France (Approval)	31 December 1990
30	European Community (Formal Confirmation)	31 December 1990
31	Yugoslavia	3 January 1991
32	Costa Rica	8 February 1991
33	Guatemala	28 February 1991
34	Madagascar (Accession)	12 March 1991
35	Oman (Accession)	15 March 1991
36	Egypt	15 March 1991
37	Monaco	23 April 1991
38	Sri Lanka (Accession)	6 June 1991
39	Myanmar (Accession)	11 June 1991
40	United Kingdom	28 June 1991
41	Venezuela	16 July 1991
42	Brazil	17 July 1991
43	Sweden	22 July 1991
44	Nepal (Accession)	24 July 1991
45	Ukraine	28 August 1991
46	Syrian Arab Republic (Accession)	3 September 1991
47	Pakistan	25 October 1991
48	Cameroon	28 October 1991
49	Cote d'Ivoire	25 November 1991
50	Portugal	3 December 1991
51	Honduras	11 December 1991
52	Denmark	19 December 1991
53	Saudi Arabia (Accession)	9 January 1992
54	Peru	16 January 1992
55	Greece	28 January 1992
56	Afghanistan	14 February 1992
57	Seychelles (Accession)	27 February 1992
58	Luxenbourg	29 April 1992
59	Burkina Faso (Accession)	2 June 1992
60	Japan	12 June 1992
61	Slovenia (Succession)	6 July 1992
62	Bulgaria	24 September 1992
63	Barbados (Accession)	15 October 1992
64	Kenya (Accession)	19 October 1992
65	Morocco	28 October 1992
66	Suriname	28 October 1992
67	Niger (Accession)	10 November 1992
68	Australia	16 November 1992
69	Iran	7 December 1992
70	Romania (Accession)	21 January 1993
71	Burundi (Accession)	18 February 1993
72	Guyana (Accession)	19 March 1993

73	Fiji (Accession)	25 March 1993
74	Antigua & Barbuda (Accession)	5 April 1993
75	Malaysia	11 May 1993
76	El Salvador (Accession)	21 May 1993
77	Zambia	28 May 1993
78	Slovakia (Succession)	28 May 1993
79	Argentina	28 June 1993
80	Dominica (Accession)	30 June 1993
81	Mauritania	1 July 1993
82	Croatia (Succession)	26 July 1993
83	Zimbabwe (Accession)	30 July 1993
84	Bosnia & Herzegovina (Succession)	1 September 1993
85	Netherlands (Acceptance)	8 September 1993
86	Dominican Republic	21 September 1993
87	Azerbaijan (Accession)	22 September 1993
88	Former Yugoslav Republic of Macedonia (Accession)	13 October 1993
89	Brunei Darussalam	12 November 1993
90	Sudan	19 November 1993
91	Germany	30 November 1993
92	Armenia (Accession)	13 December 1993
93	Czech Republic (Accession)	30 December 1993
94	Panama	13 January 1994
95	Finland (Acceptance)	15 February 1994
96	Latvia (Accession)	24 February 1994
97	St Vincent and the Grenadines (Accession)	17 May 1994
98	Poland	26 May 1994
99	Sierra Leone	6 June 1994
100	Colombia	10 June 1994
101	Kyrgzystan (Accession)	7 October 1994
102	Ethiopia	11 October 1994
103	Norway	14 November 1994
104	Moldova (Accession)	15 February 1995
105	Trinidad and Tobago	17 February 1995
106	Uruguay	10 March 1995
107	Lesotho (Accession)	28 March 1995
108	St Kitts and Nevis (Accession)	19 April 1995
109	Cape Verde (Accession)	8 May 1995
110	Algeria	9 May 1995

Appendix III

Contact List

Foreign & Commonwealth Office
Drugs and International Crime
Department
London SW1A 2AH
United Kingdom
Tel: +44 (171) 270 2436

Home Office
Head of Confiscation Section
C2 Division
International Criminal Policy
50 Queen Anne's Gate
London SW1H 9AT
United Kingdom
Tel: +44 (171) 273 3071

F3 Division
Room 412
50 Queen Anne's Gate
London SW1H 9AT
United Kingdom
Tel: +44 (171) 273 3000

C2 Division
50 Queen Anne's Gate
London SW1H 9AT
United Kingdom
Tel: +44 (171) 273 3000

Kogan Page Ltd
120 Pentonville Road
London N1 9JN
United Kingdom
Tel: +44 (171) 278 0433
Fax: +44 (171) 837 6348
Contact: Jonathan Reuvid

Mello, Hollis, Jones & Martin
Reid House
31 Church Street
Hamilton HM12
Bermuda
Tel: +1 (809) 292 1345
Fax: +1 (809) 292 2277
Contact: Saul Froomkin

Titmuss Sainer Dechert
2 Serjeant's Inn
London EC4Y 1LT
United Kingdom
Tel: +44 (171) 583 5353
Fax: +44 (171) 353 3683/2830
Contact: Rowan Bosworth-Davies

Touche Ross & Co
Forensic Services
Stonecutter Court
1 Stonecutter Street
London EC4A 4TR
United Kingdom
Tel: +44 (171) 936 3000
Fax: +44 (171) 936 2638
Contact: John Forbes

and also at

Victoria House
Vernon Place
Southampton Row
London WC1B 4DB
Tel: +44 (171) 404 6419
Fax: +44 (171) 936 2638
Contact: Martyn Jones

Professor Ernesto U Savona
Director
Research Group of Transnational Crime
School of Law
University of Trento Via Inama 5
38100 Trento
Italy
Tel: +39 (461) 882304

Addresses of Financial Regulators

Bahamas
James H Smith
The Governor
The Central Bank of the Bahamas
PO Box N4858
Nassau
Tel: +1 (809) 322 2130
Fax: +1 (809) 322 4321

Bermuda
General Manager
Bermuda Monetary Authority
Sofia Building
PO Box HM2447
48 Church Street
Hamilton HM12
Tel: +1 (809) 295 5278
Fax: +1 (809) 292 7471

British Virgin Islands
Robert Mathavious
Director of Financial Services
Financial Services Department
Government of the British Virgin
Islands
Road Town
Tortola BVI
Tel: +1 (809) 494 4190/4381
Fax: +1 (809) 494 5016

Cayman Islands
Jennifer Dilbert
Inspector of Banks and Trusts
Cayman Islands Government
Inspectorate
Grand Cayman
Tel: +1 (809) 949 7900
Fax: +1 (809) 949 7544

Cyprus
AJ Phillippou
Chief Senior Manager
Banking Supervision and Regulation
Division
Central Bank of Cyprus
80 Kennedy Avenue
Nicosia 1395
Tel: +357 (2) 379800/394395
Fax: +357 (2) 378152

Gibraltar
Financial Services Commissioner
Financial Services Commission
Suite 943
Europort PO Box 940
Tel: +350 40283/4
Fax: +350 40262

Guernsey
John Roper
Director General
Financial Services Commission
Valley House
Hirzel Street
St Peter Port
Tel: +44 (01481) 712706
Fax: +44 (01481) 712010

Hong Kong
Securities and Futures Commission
12th Floor
Edinburgh Tower
15 Queen's Road, Central
The Landmark
Tel: +852 840 9222
Fax: +852 521 7836

Ireland
The Manager
Financial Sector Department
Central Bank of Ireland
Dame Street
Dublin 2
Tel: +353 (1) 671 6666
Fax: +353 (1) 671 6561

Isle of Man
Jim Noakes
Chief Executive
Financial Services Commission
PO Box 58
1-4 Goldie Terrace
Upper Church Street
Douglas
Tel: +44 (01624) 624487
Fax: +44 (01624) 629342

Jersey
Richard Syvret
Commercial Relations Officer
Cyril Le Marquand House
The Parade
St Helier
Tel: +44 (01534) 603000
Fax: +44 (01534) 70957

Luxembourg
The IML
L-2983
Luxembourg
(banking supervision)
Tel: +352 402929 ext 221
(investment funds)
Tel: +352 402929 ext 251
Fax: +352 492180

Malta
Business Development Department
Malta Financial Services Centre
Attard
Tel: +356 441155
Fax: +356 441183

Switzerland
Supervisor of Banks and Investment
Funds
Secretariat of the Swiss Federal Banking
Commission
Markigasse 37
CH 3001 Bern
Tel: +41 (31) 161911
Fax: +41 (31) 696126

Turks and Caicos Islands
John D K Lawrence
Superintendent
Offshore Finance Centre Unit
Post Office Building
Front Street
Grand Turk
Tel: +1 (809) 946 2971
Fax: +1 (809) 946 2821

Index